Enterprise Performance Intelligence and Decision Patterns

Enterprise Performance Intelligence and Decision Patterns

Vivek Kale

CRC Press
Taylor & Francis Group
Boca Raton London New York

CRC Press is an imprint of the
Taylor & Francis Group, an **informa** business

AN AUERBACH BOOK

CRC Press
Taylor & Francis Group
6000 Broken Sound Parkway NW, Suite 300
Boca Raton, FL 33487-2742

First issued in paperback 2022

© 2018 by Vivek Kale
CRC Press is an imprint of Taylor & Francis Group, an Informa business

No claim to original U.S. Government works

ISBN 13: 978-1-03-247661-2 (pbk)
ISBN 13: 978-1-4987-8469-6 (hbk)

DOI: 10.4324/9781351228428

Library of Congress Cataloging-in-Publication Data

Names: Kale, Vivek, author.
Title: Enterprise performance intelligence and decision patterns / Vivek Kale.
Description: New York : CRC Press, [2017] | Includes bibliographical references and index.
Identifiers: LCCN 2017014535| ISBN 9781498784696 (hb : alk. paper) | ISBN 9781498784788 (e)
Subjects: LCSH: Performance technology. | Decision support systems. | Business intelligence.
Classification: LCC HF5549.5.P37 K35 2017 | DDC 658.4/032--dc23
LC record available at https://lccn.loc.gov/2017014535

Visit the Taylor & Francis Web site at
http://www.taylorandfrancis.com

and the CRC Press Web site at
http://www.crcpress.com

To Professor Jagdish N. Sheth for his guidance and support, especially during the initial stages of my career as an author and thereafter.

Contents

List of Figures

List of Tables

Preface

An inevitable consequence of organizations using the pyramid-shaped hierarchy is that there is a decision-making bottleneck at the top of the organization. The people at the top are overwhelmed by the sheer volume of decisions they have to make; they are too far away from the scene of the action to really understand what is happening; and by the time decisions are made, the measures are usually too little and too late. Consequently, companies suffer by staggering from one bad decision to another. No small group of executives, regardless of their intelligence, hard work, or sophisticated computer systems, can make all those decisions in a timely or competent manner. Given the pace of change, companies need something more agile and responsive.

The centralized command and control methods that worked for hierarchies will not work for service delivery networks. Instead of a small group of executives telling everybody else what to do, people need to be given the authority to figure out for themselves what to do. The need to be responsive to evolving customer needs and desires creates organizational structures where business intelligence (BI) and decision-making are pushed out to operating units that are closest to the scene of the action. Closed-loop decision-making resulting from a combination of ongoing performance management with ongoing BI can lead to an effective and responsive enterprise; hence, the need for performance intelligence (PI).

The effect of continuous adjustments and enhancements to business operations can generate a steady stream of savings and new revenues that may sometimes seem insignificant from one day to the next, but as months go by, may become cumulatively substantial. The profits generated in this way can be thought of as the *agility dividend*. Real-time data sharing and close coordination between business processes (sales, procurement, accounting, etc.) can be employed to deliver continuous operating adjustments that result in steady cost savings over time (negative feedback) as well as to deliver timely new products and services to identified customers that result in significant new revenue (positive feedback).

What Makes This Book Different?

A company can design and implement instruments ranging from decision patterns to PI systems that can enable continuous correction of business unit behavior in order for companies to achieve enhanced levels of productivity and profitability.

Here are the characteristic features of this book:

1. It introduces the database and related technologies such as data warehousing, data mining, analytics, and business intelligence systems that were the first step toward enabling data-driven enterprises.
2. It details decision patterns and performance decision patterns that paved the road for performance intelligence applications.
3. It enables the reader to get a clear understanding of what *performance intelligence* really means, what it might do for them, and when it is practical to use it.
4. It gives an introduction to the concepts, principles, and technologies related to performance intelligence systems (PIS).
5. It gives an introduction to the concepts and principles related to balance scorecard systems (BCS).
6. It is not focused on any particular product, platform, or service offering; it describes solutions from several commercial vendors.
7. It introduces decision patterns, that is, performance patterns in the context of performance intelligence.

This book introduces the concepts of *decision patterns* and *performance patterns* in the context of performance intelligence. Patterns are conventional solutions to recurring problems in a specific domain. Patterns originated from the area of real architecture—C. Alexander gathered architectural knowledge and best practices regarding building structures in the form of patterns. Architectural patterns capture the essential properties required for the successful design of a certain building area or function while leaving large degrees of freedom to architects.

I wanted to write a book presenting performance measurement systems in the context of the requirements arising from the development and operations of performance intelligence solutions; the outcome is the book that you are reading now. Thank you!

How Is This Book Organized?

This book traces the road to performance intelligence, the detailed features and characteristics of performance measurement systems and environments, and, in the last section, high-potential application areas of performance intelligence, namely, performance management systems, balance scorecard systems, and real-time enterprises.

Chapter 1 provides an overview of agile enterprises. Chapter 2 focuses on the alignment of IT strategy with business because that exercise helps in establishing the value drivers, critical success factors (CSF), and decision patterns of an operating enterprise that would be relevant for on-going performance intelligence.

Part I provides a glimpse of the genesis of performance management systems. Chapter 3 provides an overview of traditional decision support systems.

Part II describes significant milestones on the road to performance intelligence. Chapters 4 through 8 review the basics of databases, data warehousing, data mining, analytics, and business intelligence systems, respectively.

Part III presents a detailed discussion on various aspects of performance intelligence. Chapter 9 introduces the basic idea of decision patterns and illustrates it with a discussion of decision patterns in finance and customer relationship management. Chapter 10 employs decision patterns to define performance decision patterns. Chapter 11 introduces the concept of performance intelligence.

Part IV presents major application areas of performance intelligence: Chapter 12 discusses performance management systems, while Chapter 13 describes the balance scorecard (BSC) system. Chapter 14 presents aspects of performance intelligence for the real-time enterprises.

Who Should Read This Book?

All stakeholders in performance management and improvement projects can read this book.

This book presents a detailed discussion on various aspects of enterprise performance. The approach adopted in this book will be useful to any professional who must present a case for a performance intelligence system or to those who could be involved in a performance management or improvement project.

All readers who are involved with any aspect of a performance management project will profit by using this book as a road map to make a more meaningful contribution to the success of their project(s).

This book is addressed to those interested in:

- Enterprise performance management
- Performance intelligence
- Performance measurement and management
- Compliance management
- Decision management and optimization
- Business intelligence
- IS/ IT project management and risk management

Vivek Kale
Mumbai, India

Acknowledgments

I would like to thank all those who have helped me with their clarifications, criticism, and valuable information during the writing of this book.

Thanks again to John Wyzalek for making this book happen and guiding it through to completion.

I thank our beloved daughters, Tanaya and Atmaja, for their understanding and support. Finally, my deepest thanks and gratitude go to Girija, who has been the sounding board and critic for every thought I have had over the past years, whether good or bad, interesting or banal. She has also had the unenviable task of putting up with my periodic bouts of intensity, both in writing this book and, in life, more generally. This book simply would not exist without her help and support, and words alone cannot express my gratitude to her.

Author

Vivek Kale has more than two decades of professional IT experience during which he has handled and consulted on various aspects of enterprise-wide information modeling, enterprise architectures, business process redesign, and e-business architectures. He has been Group CIO of Essar Group, a major steel, oil, and gas company in India, as well as Raymond Ltd, a major textile and apparel company in India. He is a seasoned practitioner in transforming the business of IT, facilitating business agility, and enhancing IT-enabled enterprise intelligence. He is the author of *Big Data Computing: A Guide for Business and Technology Managers* (CRC Press 2017) and *Guide to Cloud Computing for Business and Technology Managers: From Distributed Computing to Cloudware Applications* (CRC Press 2015).

Other Books by Vivek Kale

Inverting the Paradox of Excellence: How Companies Use Variations for Business Excellence and How Enterprise Variations Are Enabled by SAP (CRC Press, 2015).

Implementing SAP® CRM: The Guide for Business and Technology Managers (CRC Press, 2015).

Enhancing Enterprise Intelligence: Leveraging ERP, CRM, SCM, PLM, BPM, and BI (CRC Press, 2016).

Agile Network Businesses: Collaboration, Coordination, and Competitive Advantage (CRC Press, 2017).

1

DATA-DRIVEN PERFORMANCE

1.1 Agile Enterprises

The difficult challenges facing businesses today require enterprises to be transitioned into flexible, agile structures that can respond to new market opportunities quickly with a minimum of new investment and risk. As enterprises have experienced the need to be simultaneously efficient, flexible, responsive, and adaptive, they have transitioned themselves into agile enterprises with small, autonomous teams that work concurrently and reconfigure quickly, and adopt highly decentralized management that recognizes its knowledge base and manages it effectively.

Enterprise agility is the ability to be:

1. Responsive. Adaptability is enabled by the concept of loosely coupled interacting components reconfigurable within a unified framework. This is essential for ensuring opportunity management to sustain viability.

   The ability to be responsive involves the following aspects:
   - An organizational structure that enables change which is based on reusable elements that are reconfigurable in a scalable framework. Reusability and reconfigurability are generic concepts that are applicable to work procedures, manufacturing cells, production teams or information automation systems.
   - An organizational culture that facilitates change and focuses on change proficiency.
2. Intelligence intensive or able to manage and apply knowledge effectively whether it is knowledge of a customer, a market opportunity, a competitor's threat, a production process, a business practice, a product technology, or an individual's competency. This is essential for ensuring innovation management to sustain leadership.

The ability to be intelligence intensive involves the following aspects:

- Enterprise knowledge management
- Enterprise collaborative learning

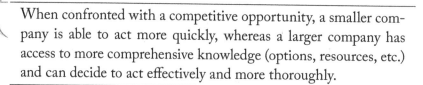

When confronted with a competitive opportunity, a smaller company is able to act more quickly, whereas a larger company has access to more comprehensive knowledge (options, resources, etc.) and can decide to act effectively and more thoroughly.

Agility is the ability to respond to (and ideally benefit from) unexpected change. It is unplanned and unscheduled adaption to unforeseen and unexpected external circumstances. However, we must differentiate between agility and flexibility. Flexibility is scheduled or planned adaptation to unforeseen yet expected external circumstances.

One of the foremost abilities of an agile enterprise is its ability to quickly react to change and adapt to new opportunities. This ability to change works along two dimensions:

1. The number or "types of change" an enterprise is able to undergo
2. The "degree of change" an enterprise is able to undergo

The former is termed range and the latter is termed response ability. The more *response able* an enterprise is, the more radical a change it can address gracefully. Range refers to how large a domain is covered by the agile response system; in other words, how far from the expected set of events one can go and still have the system respond well. However, given a specific range, how well the system responds is a measure of response or change ability.

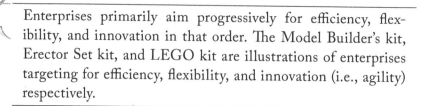

Enterprises primarily aim progressively for efficiency, flexibility, and innovation in that order. The Model Builder's kit, Erector Set kit, and LEGO kit are illustrations of enterprises targeting for efficiency, flexibility, and innovation (i.e., agility) respectively.

Construction toys offer a useful metaphor because the enterprise systems we are concerned with must be configured and reconfigured constantly, which is precisely the objective of most construction toys. An enterprise system architecture and structure consisting of reusable components reconfigurable in a scalable framework can be an effective base model for creating variable (or built-for-change) systems. For achieving this, the nature of the framework appears to be a critical factor. We can introduce the framework/component concept by looking at three types of construction toys and observing how they are used in practice, namely erector set, LEGO, and Model Builder's kits.

You can build virtually anything over and over again with any of these toys, but fundamental differences in their architectures give each system unique dynamic characteristics. All these systems consist of a basic set of core construction components, and also have an architectural and structural framework that enables connecting the components into a huge variety of configurations. Nevertheless, the model builder is not as reusable in practice as the erector set and the erector set is not as reusable, reconfigurable or scalable in practice as LEGO, but LEGO is more reusable, reconfigurable, and scalable than either of the other two. LEGO is the dominant construction toy of choice among preteen builders who appear to value experimentation and innovation.

The Model Builder's kit can be used to construct one object like an airplane of one intended size. As a highly integrated system, this construction kit offers maximum esthetic appeal for one-time construction use; but the parts are not reusable, the construction cannot be reconfigured, and one intended size precludes any scalability. However, it will remain what it is for all time—there is zero variability here.

Erector Set kits can be purchased for constructing specific models, such as a small airplane that can be assembled in many different configurations. With the Erector Set kit, the first built model is likely to remain as originally configured in any particular play session. The erector set, for all its modular structure, is just not as reconfigurable in practice as LEGO. The erector set connectivity framework employs a special-purpose intermediate subsystem used solely to attach one part to another, for instance a nut-and-bolt pair and a 90-degree elbow. The components in the system all have holes through which the bolts may pass to connect one component with another. When a nut is lost, a bolt is useless, and vice versa. And when all the nuts and bolts remaining in a set have been used, any remaining construction components are useless, and vice versa. All the parts in a LEGO set can always be used and reused, but an erector set, for all its modularity, is not as reusable in practice as LEGO.

LEGO offers similar kits, and both toys (LEGO and Erector Set) include a few necessary special parts, like wheels and cowlings, to augment the core construction components. Watch a child work with either and you'll see the LEGO construction undergoes constant metamorphosis; the child may start with one of the pictured configurations, but then reconfigure the pieces into all manner of other imagined styles. LEGO components are plug-compatible with each other, incorporating the connectivity framework as an integral feature of the component. A standard grid of bumps and cavities on component surfaces allows them to snap together into a larger configuration—without limit.

A Model Builder's kit has a tight framework: a precise construction sequence, no part interchangeability, and high integration. An erector set has a loose framework that does not encourage interaction among parts and insufficiently discriminates among compatible parts. In contrast, each component in the LEGO system carries all it needs to interact with other components (the interaction framework rejects most unintended parts), and can grow without end.

1.1.1 Stability versus Agility

Most large-scale change efforts in established enterprises fail to meet expectations because nearly all models of organization design, effectiveness, and change assume stability is not only desirable but also attainable. The theory and practice in organization design explicitly encourage organizations to seek alignment, stability, and equilibrium. The predominant logic of organizational effectiveness has been that an organization's fit with its environment, its execution, and its predictability are the keys to its success. Organizations are encouraged to institutionalize best practices, freeze them into place, focus on execution, stick to their knitting, increase predictability, and get processes under control. These ideas establish stability as the key to performance.

The stability of a distinctive competitive advantage is a strong driver for organization design because of its expected link to excellence and effectiveness. Leveraging an advantage requires commitments that focus attention, resources, and investments on the chosen alternatives. In other words, competitive advantage results when enterprises finely hone their operations to perform in a particular way. This leads to large investments in operating technologies, structures, and ways of doing things. If such commitments are successful, they lead to a period of high performance and a considerable amount of positive reinforcement. Financial markets reward stable competitive advantages and predictable streams of earnings: a commitment to alignment reflects a commitment to stability.

Consequently, enterprises are built to support stable strategies, organizational structures, and enduring value creations, not to vary. For example, the often-used strengths, weaknesses, opportunities, and threats (SWOT) analysis encourages firms to leverage opportunities while avoiding weaknesses and threats. This alignment among positive and negative forces is implicitly assumed to remain constant, and there is no built-in assumption of agility. When environments are stable or at least predictable, enterprises are characterized by rules, norms, and systems that limit experimentation, control variation, and reward consistent performance. They have many checks and balances in place to ensure that the organization operates in the prescribed manner. Thus, to get the high performance, enterprises put in place practices they see as a good fit, without considering whether they can be changed and whether they will support changes in future, that is, by aligning themselves to achieve high performance today, enterprises often make it difficult to vary so that they can have high performance tomorrow.

When the environment is changing slowly or predictably, these models are adequate. However, as the rate of change increases with increasing globalization, technological breakthroughs, associative alliances, and regulatory changes, enterprises have to look for greater agility, flexibility, and innovation from their companies. Instead of pursuing strategies, structures, and cultures that are designed to create long-term competitive advantages, companies must seek a string of temporary competitive advantages through an approach to organization design that assumes change is normal. With the advent of the

Internet and the accompanying extended "virtual" market spaces, enterprises are now competing based on intangible assets like identity, intellectual property, ability to attract and retain customers, and their ability to organize, reorganize frequently, or organize differently in different areas depending on the need. Thus, the need for change in management and organization is much more frequent, and excellence is much more a function of possessing the ability to change. Enterprises need to be built around practices that encourage change, not thwart it. Instead of having to create change efforts, disrupt the status quo, or adapt to change, enterprises should be built-for-change.

To meet the conflicting objectives of performing well against the current set of environmental demands and changing themselves to face future business environments, enterprises must engender two types of changes: the natural process of evolution, or what we will call strategic adjustments, and strategic reorientations.

1. Strategic adjustments involve the day-to-day tactical changes required to bring in new customers, make incremental improvements in products and services, and comply with regulatory requirements. This type of change helps fine-tune current strategies and structures to achieve short-term results; it is steady, incremental, and natural. This basic capability to evolve is essential if an enterprise is to survive to thrive.

2. Strategic reorientation involves altering an existing strategy and, in some cases, adopting a new strategy. When the environment evolves or changes sufficiently, an enterprise must significantly adjust some elements of its strategy and the way it executes that strategy. More often than not, enterprises have to face a transformational change that involves not just a new strategy but a transformation of the business model that leads to new products, services, and customers, and requires markedly new competencies and capabilities. However, operationally all these changes can be seen as manifestations of the basic changes, only differing in degree and number of dimensions.

Maintaining an agile enterprise is not a matter of searching for the strategy but continuously strategizing, not a matter of specifying an organization design but committing to a process of organizing, and not generating value but continuously improving the efficiency and effectiveness of the value generation process. It is a search for a series of temporary configurations that create short-term advantages. In turbulent environments, enterprises that string together a series of temporary but adequate competitive advantages will outperform enterprises that stick with one advantage for an extended period of time. The key issue for the built-for-change enterprise is orchestration, or coordinating the multiple changing subsystems to produce high levels of current enterprise performance.

1.1.2 Aspects of Agility

This section addresses the analytical side of agility or change proficiency of the enterprise. It highlights the fundamental principles that underlie an enterprise's ability to change, and by indicating how to apply these principles in real situations, it illustrates what it is that makes a business and any of its constituting systems easy to change.

Agility or change proficiency enables both efficiency programs (e.g., lean production) and transformation programs. If the enterprise is proficient at change, it can adapt to take advantage of an unpredictable opportunity and can also counter the unpredictable threat. Agility can embrace semantics across the whole spectrum: it can capture cycle-time reduction, with everything happening faster; it can build on lean production, with high resource productivity; it can encompass mass customization, with customer responsive product variation; it can embrace virtual enterprise, with streamlined supplier networks and opportunistic partnerships; it can echo reengineering, with a process and transformation focus; and it can demand a learning organization, with systemic training and education. Being agile means being proficient at change. Agility allows an enterprise to do anything it wants to do whenever it wants to—or has to—do it. Thus, an agile enterprise can employ business process reengineering as a core competency when transformation is called for; it can hasten its conversion to lean production when greater efficiencies are useful; it can continue to succeed when constant innovation becomes the dominant competitive strategy. Agility can be wielded overtly as a business strategy as well as inherently as a sustainable-existence competency.

Agility derives from both the physical ability to act (change ability) and the intellectual ability to find appropriate things to act on (knowledge management). Agility can be expressed as the ability to manage and apply knowledge effectively so that enterprise has the potential to thrive in a continuously changing and unpredictable business environment. Agility derives from two sources: an enterprise architecture that enables change and an organizational culture that facilitates change. The enterprise architecture that enables change is based on reusable elements that are reconfigurable in a scalable framework.

Agility is a core fundamental requirement of all enterprises. It was not an area of interest when environmental change was relatively slow and predictable. Now there is virtually no choice; enterprises must develop a conscious competency. Practically all enterprises now need some method to assess their agility and determine whether it is sufficient or needs improvement. This section introduces techniques for characterizing, measuring, and comparing variability in all aspects of business and among different businesses.

1.1.3 Principles of Agile Systems

Christopher Alexander introduced the concept of patterns in the late 1970s in the field of architecture. A pattern describes a commonly occurring solution that generates decidedly successful outcomes.

A list of success patterns for agile enterprises (and systems) in terms of their constituting elements or functions or components is given below.

1. Reusable

    Agility Pattern 1 Self-Contained Units (Components): *The components of agile enterprises are autonomous units cooperating toward a shared goal.*

    Agility Pattern 2 Plug Compatibility: *The components of agile enterprises are reusable and multiply replicable, that is, depending on requirements multiple instances of the same component can be invoked concurrently.*

    Agility Pattern 3 Facilitated Reuse: *The components of agile enterprises share well-defined interaction and interface standards, and can be inserted, removed, and replaced easily and noninvasively.*

2. Reconfigurable

Agility Pattern 4 Flat Interaction: *The components of agile enterprises communicate, coordinate, and cooperate with other components concurrently and in real-term sharing of current, complete, and consistent information on interactions with individual customers.*

Agility Pattern 5 Deferred Commitment: *The components of agile enterprises establish relationships with other components in the real term to enable deferment of customer commitment to as late a stage as possible within the sales cycle, coupled with the corresponding ability to postpone the point of product differentiation as close as possible to the point of purchase by the customer.*

Agility Pattern 6 Distributed Control and Information: *The components of agile enterprises are defined declaratively rather than procedurally; the network of components displays the defining characteristics of any "small worlds" network, namely local robustness and global accessibility.*

Agility Pattern 7 Self-organization: *The components of agile enterprises are self-aware and they interact with other components via on-the-fly integration, adjustment, or negotiation.*

3. Scalable

Agility Pattern 8 Evolving Standards (Framework): *The components of agile enterprises operate within predefined frameworks that standardize intercomponent communication and interaction, determine component compatibility, and evolve to accommodate old, current, and new components.*

Agility Pattern 9 Redundancy and Diversity: *The components of agile enterprises replicate components to provide the desired capacity, load-balancing and performance, fault tolerance as well as variations on the basic component functionality and behavior.*

Agility Pattern 10 Elastic Capacity: *The components of agile enterprises enable dynamic utilization of additional or a reduced number of resources depending on the requirements.*

1.1.4 Framework for Agile Proficiency

How do we measure enterprise agility? This section establishes a metric framework for proficiency at change. An enterprise's change proficiency may exist in one or more dimensions of changes. These dimensions of changes can form a structural framework for understanding current capabilities and setting strategic priorities for improvement: How does the agile enterprise know when it is improving its changeability, or losing ground? How does it know if it is less changeable than its competition? How does it set improvement targets? Thus, a practical measure of change proficiency is needed before we can talk meaningfully about getting more of it, or even getting some of it.

It must be highlighted that measuring change competency is generally not unidimensional, nor likely to result in an absolute and unequivocal comparative metric. Change proficiency has both reactive and proactive modes. Reactive change is opportunistic and responds to a situation that threatens viability. Proactive change is innovative and responds to a possibility for leadership. An enterprise sufficiently proficient at reactive change when prodded should be able to use that competency proactively and let others do the reacting.

Would it be proficient if a short-notice change was completed in the time required, but at a cost that eventually bankrupted the company? Or if the changed environment thereafter required the special wizardry and constant attention of a specific employee to keep it operational? Is it proficient if the change is virtually free and painless, but out-of-synch with market opportunity timing? Is it proficient if it can readily accommodate a broad latitude of change that is no longer needed, or too narrow for the latest challenges thrown at it by the business environment? Are we change proficient if we can accommodate any change that comes our way as long as it is within a narrow 10 percent of where we already are?

Therefore, change proficiency can be understood to be codetermined by four parameters:

- Time: a measure of elapsed time to complete a change (fairly objective)
- Cost: a measure of monetary cost incurred in a change (somewhat objective)
- Quality: a measure of prediction quality in meeting change time, cost, and specification targets robustly (somewhat subjective)
- Range: a measure of the latitude of possible change, typically defined and determined by mission or charter (fairly subjective)

1.2 Data-Driven Performance Management

The history of change has always been driven by innovation and technology, an idea encapsulated in the term "creative destruction" coined by Joseph Schumpeter, an Austrian-American economist, in *Capitalism, Socialism and Democracy*. He argued that the constant evolution of industries revolutionizes the very economic structure they are part of, continually destroying it and creating a new one. The advent of the information age we live in today represents this process in high definition. The rise of information technology has a huge impact on industries, bringing with it greater opportunities and greater risks. Reflect on the downfall of big names such as Kodak, Blockbuster, or Borders and the rise of Apple, Amazon, Google, and Facebook. Those organizations finding new ways of creating and leveraging information are ruling our time. Those that cannot adapt suffer a Darwinian extinction. At the heart of this story is the emergence of data and analytics as the means to drive business.

Performance intelligence is about embedding analytics within business processes and automating decisions so that thousands or millions of decisions every day are made by analytics processes without any human intervention. Whether those decisions directly touch customers or simply optimize an organization's actions behind the scenes, the impact can be substantial. If an organization does not begin to move toward performance intelligence, it will struggle as its competitors drive analytics deeper into their business processes. The myriad performance intelligence opportunities available to businesses today are driven by increased data availability, increased analytics processing horsepower, and increased accessibility of robust analytics techniques.

Organizations gain advantages when performance intelligence is integrated into a system. They gain actionable insight and the ability to link strategies to plans, continuously monitor execution against goals, and drive higher levels of performance. They can share goals and progress with the individuals responsible for achieving them. And individuals can share insight and information with management and their peers to ensure alignment.

1.3 Summary

This chapter discussed the need and characteristics of agile enterprises. It presented various strategies adopted for enabling enterprise agility ranging from e-business transformations to mobilizing the business processes.

2

ALIGNING BUSINESS AND IT STRATEGY

Strategic management, as the process of business strategy formulation and strategy implementation, is concerned with establishing goals and directions, and developing and carrying out plans to achieve those goals. As organizations evolve, so do their strategies and strategic management practices. In recent years, information technology (IT) has become increasingly important in strategic management. IT and IT-enabled systems are now indispensable in supporting business strategies.

The value of information and knowledge has far surpassed that of physical goods. Information resources have become a key differentiator of successful businesses. Companies that manage information well are more likely to maintain a competitive advantage against their peers. Because information has become a major force in driving business activities, every business is in the information business.

In the early days, IT's contribution to the organization was largely information provision, monitoring, and control. IT and information systems (IS) are now integrated into almost every aspect of business, from planning to analysis and design, operations management and strategic decision-making. Even for those businesses not in information industries, information plays a vital role in supporting their business functions, from strategizing to routine operations.

IT and IS have experienced dramatic changes in the last few decades. Their major role in business has shifted from tools to support "back-office" operations to an integrated part of business strategies and the maintenance of core competencies. Strategic management, as the process of business strategy formulation and strategy implementation, is concerned with establishing goals and directions, and developing and carrying out plans to achieve those goals. As organizations evolve, so do their strategies and strategic management practices.

In recent years, IT has become increasingly important in strategic management. IT and IT-enabled systems are now indispensable in supporting business strategies.

2.1 Business Strategy

2.1.1 Evolution of Strategy Management

Strategic management is concerned with managerial decisions and actions that determine the long-term prosperity of the organization. An organization must have a clear strategy and its strategy must be carefully developed and implemented to match its resources and environment in the pursuit of its organizational goals. Two meanings behind the often-used term "strategy" are the ideational content of strategy and the process of formulating this strategy. The former refers to the array of options that one uses to compete and survive, and the latter refers to the planning that leads to the construction of the strategic plan. Thus, IT-enabled strategic management addresses the role IT plays in strategy content options and priorities, strategy formulation processes and strategy implementation processes. Strategic management focuses on identifying the direction of an organization, and designing and instituting major changes needed to gear the organization toward moving in the established direction. The presentation and approach in this subsection has been adopted from Z. Tang and B. Walters (2009).

Early research in strategic management started in the 1950s, with leading researchers such as Peter Drucker, Alfred Chandler, and Philip Selznick. Drucker pioneered the theory of management by objectives (MBO). He is also one of the first to recognize the dramatic changes IT brought to management. He predicted in the 1960s the rise of knowledge workers in the information age. Alfred Chandler recognized the importance of a corporate-level strategy that gives a business its structure and direction; as he put it, *structure follows strategy*. Philip Selznick established the groundwork of matching a company's internal attributes with external factors.

In the 1970s, theories of strategic management primarily focused on growth, market share, and portfolio analysis. A long-term study aimed at understanding the Profit Impact of Marketing Strategies (PIMS) was carried out from the 1960s to the 1970s. The study concluded that as a result of economies of scale, a company's rate of profit is positively correlated with its market share. As companies pursued larger market share, a number of growth strategies—such as horizontal integration, vertical integration, diversification, franchises, mergers and acquisitions, and joint ventures—were developed. As will be discussed later, those strategies are even more widely used today, with the facilitation of networking and information technologies. Another shifting of strategic focus occurring in the 1970s was the move from sales orientation toward customer orientation. Theodore Levitt argued that businesses should start with the customer proposition. Rather than creating a product and then trying to sell it to customers, the right approach is to find out how to create value for customers and then make the products and services that meet the needs of the customers.

In the 1980s, strategic management theories were largely geared toward gaining competitive advantages. Michael Porter proposed a number of very influential strategic analysis models, such as the five-force model of competition, the value chain and generic competitive strategies. Porter suggested that businesses need to choose either a strategy of cost leadership (with lowest cost), product differentiation, or market focus. Adopting one of Porter's generic strategies helps a company to avoid the so-called stuck-in-the-middle problem. Many of Porter's ideas have been implemented in modern corporate strategic management frameworks.

Strategic IS applications, such as supply chain management, are based on efficient value chain management and forming strategic alliances to maintain competitive advantages.

R. Lester suggested that companies sustain their strategic positions in the market by following seven best practices: continuously improving products and services, breaking down barriers between functional areas, flattening organizational hierarchies, strengthening relationships with customers and suppliers, effectively using technology, having a global orientation, and enhancing human resource quality. Various information technologies have been used to support those best practices.

G. Hamel and C. K. Prahalad popularized the idea of core competencies. They argued that companies should devote their resources to a few things that they can do better than the competition, and relegate noncore business operations to business partners. This laid the foundation for outsourcing, which has gained in popularity since the late 1990s.

The wide spread use of network and information technologies has reduced the time and geographic barriers of outsourcing business functions to other companies.

Reengineering, also known as business process redesign, calls for fundamental changes in the way business is carried out. Traditional companies are organized around functional business areas, which often leads to limited communication and cooperation, as well as redundancy due to functional overlap. Michael Hammer and James Champy's book *Reengineering the Corporation* makes a convincing case for restructuring business resources around whole business processes rather than functional tasks. IT and IS have become both an impetus and a facilitator for reengineering projects and efforts.

In the 1990s, researchers increasingly recognized the importance of customer relationship management. Computer and network technologies have played a key role in making customer relationship management efficient and effective. Along the line of improving value to the customers, mass customization provides competitive advantages. Reaching and custom-serving individual customers are only feasible with the proliferation of information and communication technologies.

Peter Senge, in his book *The Fifth Discipline*, popularized the concept of the learning organization. The rationale for creating a learning organization is that the business environment has become more dynamic and complex. Companies must have the ability to learn continuously and adapt to the changing environment. People in a learning organization need to continuously expand their capacity to become more productive or to maintain their level of competency.

Recently, many researchers have recognized that organizations are complex adaptive systems in which multiple agents set their own goals, share information, collaborate, and interact with one another (V. Kale 2017).

2.1.2 Sustaining Competitive Advantage

Competitive advantage is an advantage that a firm has over its competitors, allowing it to generate greater sales or margins and/or retain more customers than its competition. There can be many types of competitive advantages including the firm's cost structure, product offerings, distribution network, and customer support and information systems. Different organizations evolve and adopt different strategies to seek competitive advantage, and different strategies in turn result in different competitive advantages. Competitive advantages give a company an edge over its rivals and an ability to generate greater value for the firm and its shareholders. The more sustainable the competitive advantage, the more difficult it is for competitors to neutralize the advantage.

Competitive advantage can be defined as *a product or service that an organization's customers value more highly than similar offerings from its competitors*. Competitive advantages are typically temporary as competitors often seek ways to duplicate the competitive advantage. In order to stay ahead of competition, organizations have to continually renew or develop new competitive advantages.

Competitive advantage is the favorable position an organization seeks in order to be more profitable than its competitors. It involves communicating a greater perceived value to a target market than its competitors can provide. This can be achieved through many avenues including offering a better-quality product or service, lowering prices and increasing marketing efforts. Sustainable competitive advantage refers to maintaining a favorable position over the long term, which can help boost a company's image in the marketplace, its valuation and its future earning potential. Porter maintains that achieving competitive advantage requires a firm to make a choice about the type and scope of its competitive advantage.

There are two main types of competitive advantage: comparative advantage and differential advantage:

- Comparative advantage, or cost advantage, is a firm's ability to produce a good or service at a lower cost than its competitors, which gives the firm the ability sell its goods or services at a lower price than its competition or to generate a larger margin on sales.
- Differential advantage is created when a firm's products or services differ from its competitors and are seen as better than a competitor's products by customers.

Organizations can analyze, identify, and develop competitive advantages using tools such as Porter's Five Forces, three generic strategies and value chains.

2.1.2.1 Porter's Five Forces Model   Michael Porter's Five Forces Model is a useful tool to assist in assessing the competition in an industry and determining the relative attractiveness of that industry. In order to carry out an industry analysis, a firm must analyze five competitive forces:

1. Rivalry of competitors within its industry
2. Threat of new entrants into an industry and its markets
3. Threat posed by substitute products which might capture market share
4. Bargaining power of customers
5. Bargaining power of suppliers

2.1.2.2 Porter's Framework of Generic Strategies   To survive and succeed, a business must develop and implement strategies to effectively counter the above five competitive forces. The most widely known strategy framework is the three generic strategies introduced by Michael Porter. Subsequently, Porter added a further aspect to his model: whether the strategic target is industrywide or focused on a particular segment.

The three generic competitive strategies are:

1. The overall cost leadership strategy dictates that the firm construct efficient and appropriately scaled facilities, pursue cost reduction based on the experience curve, and tightly control direct costs and overheads. Even though lower cost relative to competitors is the major strategic target, a watchful eye must be placed on quality, service and customer satisfaction. Achieving overall cost leadership yields above-average returns due to the lower costs, while competitors have competed away their profits.
2. The differentiation strategy dictates that the firm create a product offering that is perceived industrywide as being unique. The differentiation can take many forms: design, brand, technology, features, customer service, dealer network, and many more.

The firm differentiates itself along several dimensions. While costs are not allowed to be ignored, they are not the primary strategic target. If differentiation is achieved, above-average returns can be obtained due to the defensible position it creates. Differentiation has proven to be a viable strategy resulting in brand loyalty and lower sensitivity to price.

Characteristics of the differentiation strategy are

- Margins that avoid the urge for a low-cost position
- Decreased buyer power due to a lack of comparable alternatives
- Entry barriers for competitors

3. The focus strategy dictates that the firm cater to a particular segment only (e.g., one particular buyer group, geographic market, etc.). It bases its above-average returns on serving a particular target very well, that is, more efficiently than competitors competing more broadly. A focus strategy either achieves differentiation by better meeting the needs and wants of the particular target it focuses on, or manages to maintain lower costs in serving this target, or both. The differentiation or lower cost position is not achieved for the entire market but only for the narrow market target.

Although initially cost leadership and differentiation were regarded as being incompatible, subsequently hybrid competitive strategies combining the above strategies were explored. While the generic hybrid strategies (high relative differentiation/high relative cost position, and low relative differentiation/low relative cost position) were only ascribed an average competitive position, the combination of high relative differentiation position and a low relative cost position was considered powerful. The strategy resulting from such a hybrid combination of differentiation (customization) and cost leadership (standardization) is called *mass customization*.

Information technology can be a critical enabler for an extended set of five generic strategies:

1. *Cost leadership*: Organizations can use information systems to fundamentally shift the cost of doing business or reduce the costs of business processes and/or lower the costs of engaging customers or suppliers, that is, using online

business-to-consumer (B2C) and business-to-business (B2B) models, and e-procurement systems to reduce operating costs.

2. *Differentiation*: Organizations can use information systems to develop differentiated features and/or to reduce competitors' differentiation advantages, that is, using online live chat systems and social networks to better understand and serve customers; using technology to create infomediaries to offer value-added service and improve customers' stickiness to your website/business; and applying advanced and established measures for online operations to off-line practices (i.e., more accurate and systematic ways of measuring the efficiency and effectiveness of advertising).

3. *Innovation*: Organizations can use information systems to identify and create (or assist in creating) new products and services and/or to develop new/niche markets and/or to radically change business processes via automation (i.e., using digital modeling and simulation of product design to reduce the time and cost to the market). They also can work on new initiatives to establish pure online businesses/operations. Everyone is connected via personal computers, laptops, and other mobile devices through cabled internet or wireless or mobile networks, so there are plenty of opportunities to co-create with customers, external partners, and internal staff. The internet and telecommunications networks provide better capabilities and opportunities for innovation. There are a large number of component parts on the networks that are very expensive or were extremely disparate before the networks were established, and organizations could combine or recombine these components/parts to create new innovations.

4. *Growth (including mergers and acquisitions)*: Organizations can use information systems to expand domestic and international operations and/or to diversify and integrate into other products and services, that is, establish global intranet and global operation platforms; establish omni-channel strategy to gain growth (omni-channel strategy looks at leveraging the advantages of both online [or digital] and off-line [or nondigital] channels).

5. *Strategic alliance*: Organizations can use information systems to create and enhance relations with partners via applications, such as developing virtual organizations and interorganizational information systems.

Supplementary strategies enabled by information systems are:

1. Raising barriers to entry through improving operations and/or optimizing/flattening organizational structure by increasing the amount or the complexity of the technology required (e.g. Google's search engine and Proctor & Gamble's digitization strategy which make it the world's most technologically enabled firm).
2. Building switching costs via extranets and proprietary software applications (e.g., Amazon's user-friendly and useful B2C website).
3. Locking in customers or suppliers by enhancing relationships and building valuable new relationships via customer/partner relationship management systems/applications (i.e., providing a bank's customers with multiple touch points via telephones, the internet, fax machines, videos, mobile devices, ATMs, branches, the bank's agents).

2.1.2.3 Porter's Value Chain The value chain approach views an organization as a chain, or series, of processes, and it classifies an organization's activities into two categories: primary activities (i.e., inbound logistics, operations, sales and marketing, customer service, outbound logistics) and secondary/support activities (i.e., administration, human resources, technology, procurement). The value chain helps an organization to determine the value of its business processes for its customers. The model highlights specific activities in the business where competitive strategies can be best applied.

Value chain is an important concept and tool that can help a business identify competitive advantage and opportunities for strategic use of information systems. By creating/adding value and thus creating competitive advantages, information systems could contribute to each part of an organization's value chain and extended value chain (including interactions/ties with external partners and strategic alliances):

- By leveraging on internet technologies, organizations could also create a value web or a hub structure, both of which could improve the efficiency and effectiveness of the value chain and supply chain
- By digitally connecting customers, suppliers, and partners; by reducing the information gaps/errors along the chain (especially demand and supply)
- By bettering communication, cooperation, and collaboration

2.2 Information Technology and Information Systems (IT/IS)

Strategic management and IT/IS have progressed along their separate paths, but there are many instances where their paths have converged. The motivation of IS has shifted from efficiency to effectiveness, and in the internet era, to value creation. On the one hand, IT is playing a more active and important role in strategic management. On the other hand, strategic management concerns have influenced the development of IS. In many cases, the theories and principles of strategic management led the way for IS development. IT and IS, in turn, have made it more feasible for those theories and principles to be put into practice in businesses. The presentation and approach in the next couple of subsections is adapted from Z. Tang and B. Walters (2009).

2.2.1 Evolution of IT

The short history of computer IT development can be divided into three eras:

- the mainframe era from the 1950s to the 1970s
- the microcomputer era from the 1980s to the early 1990s,
- the internet era from the 1990s to the present.

The mainframe era was characterized by centralized computing, where all computing needs were serviced by powerful computers at a computer center. The proliferation of microcomputers led to decentralized computing. Computing resources become readily accessible to more users. This is a period that witnessed improved user performance and decision-making quality. When computer networks became pervasive in the internet era, decentralized computing evolved to distributed computing, where computing resources are located in multiple sites, as in decentralized systems, but all of the computing resources are connected through computer networks. People in the internet era are far more empowered than in previous eras, because they have access not only to technology tools as before, but also to shared knowledge from others. Assuming bilateral interaction, the value of a network increases with the square of the number of users connected to the network. The wide accessibility of the internet has created numerous opportunities for businesses and brought fundamental changes to the way businesses operate.

One of the milestones in the computer industry was the arrival of the IBM System/360 in 1964 running the same operating systems and using the same peripherals. Thus, companies could start with a lower configuration model and, with increasing requirements, expand capacity with more powerful models without the need to replace system software and peripheral components. Easy adoption through inter-changeability of hardware and software prompted significant growth of computer system usage in businesses in the 1960s and 1970s. IBM first started unbundling software from hardware by selling software separate from its computer in 1969. That set the stage for the launch of an independent software industry. The fast growth of packaged software applications, in turn, spurred the growth of computer hardware.

The next major event in the computer industry was the birth of personal computers (PCs) in the mid-1970s. Intel introduced the first semiconductor microchip (the Intel 4004) in 1971. However, PCs were not widespread until the early 1980s, when IBM launched its standardized PC (known as the IBM PC). The IBM PC became "Machine of the Year," taking the place of traditional "Man of the Year" on the cover of *Time* magazine in 1983. Other computer vendors jumped on the IBM PC bandwagon by producing IBM-compatible PCs. During the decade of the 1980s, the number of PCs grew from more than 100-fold to more than 100 million.

Low-cost computing changed organizational computing architecture from centralized computing to distributed computing systems in the 1980s. Once scarce and expensive, computer systems are now abundant and inexpensive because of the availability of desktop computers, laptop computers, and even handheld computing devices enabled by the relentless progress dictated by Moore's law. The continued growth of the PC industry is driven by the well-known Moore's law, which stipulates that the number of transistors per silicon chip doubles roughly every 18 months, and hence, the corresponding performance of the central processing unit—the brain of microcomputers. Moore's law has remained valid for the last six decades. The power of exponential growth resulted in a dramatic cost and performance improvement in computer hardware.

In the history of IT, the 1990s is perhaps best known as the decade of the Internet boom. The internet started as the U.S. Department of Defense's ARPAnet, with the aim of creating a distributed computer network that could withstand a nuclear attack. In the 1970s and 1980s, the internet was used mainly by academics and scientists, and was not generally accessible by the general public because its use, although open, required substantial knowledge of specific application protocols. Two major events led to the explosive growth of the Internet:

1. The first was the development of the world-wide web (WWW or the Web) by Tim Berners-Lee, a researcher at CERN in Switzerland in 1990. The web made it possible to link information resources all over the world through the Internet. Users could retrieve information without knowing the *location* of the information by simply following the hyperlinks (or links).

2. The second was the arrival of a graphic browser. Initial access to the WWW was text based and so its content and usability were limited. The WWW took off after 1993 when the first graphic web browser, Mosaic, was released by the National Center for Supercomputing Applications (NCSA) at the University of Illinois at Urbana Champaign. The ensuing Internet growth was unprecedented in the history of technology development. Internet users grew from a few thousand

to more than 300 million during the 1990s. As of June 2016, there were more than 3.6 billion Internet users worldwide (www.internetworldstats.com/stats.htm). The internet provides a low-cost way of connecting virtually everyone in modern society to an open and shared common network.

Since the late 1990s, mobile computing based on wireless network technologies has gained a lot of momentum. Intelligent appliances, such as cellular phones, personal digital assistants and other handheld computing devices, became a significant part of the IS infrastructure. IDC predicts that the number of devices connected to the Internet will surpass 20 billion by 2020. Ubiquitous computing that allows *anytime, anyplace* access to information resources will bring dramatic changes to the business environment.

The next major development of the Web was network intelligence through Web Services. The nonprofit Internet governing organization W3C defines Web Services as programmatic interfaces for application-to-application communication on the web. Web services create a promising infrastructure to support loosely coupled, distributed and heterogeneous applications on the internet. Applications based on web services can be described, published, located, and invoked over the internet to create new products and services based on open internet protocols such as HTTP, XML, and Simple Object Access Protocol (SOAP). The significance of Web Services is that system-to-system communications can be automated; hence, building business alliances and virtual organizations becomes much easier than with current internet technology (V. Kale 2015).

2.2.2 Evolution of IS

The role of business IS has evolved and expanded over the last six decades. Early systems in the 1950s and 1960s were used primarily for dealing with business transactions with associated data collection, processing, and storage. Management information systems (MIS) were developed in the 1960s to provide information for managerial support. Typical MIS are report based, with little or no decision-making support capabilities. Decision support systems (DSS) first appeared in the 1970s. They offer various analytical tools, models and flexible user interfaces for decision support for solving difficult problems, such as planning, forecasting, and scheduling. Executive support systems (ESS) are specialized DSS designed to support top-level management in strategic decision-making.

A strategic information system include any type of IS that plays a key role in supporting business strategies. McFarlan's strategic grid defines four categories of IT impact: support, factory, turnaround and strategic. When the IT has a significant impact on business core strategy, core operations or both, the corresponding IS are considered strategic information systems.

The 1990s saw an increased emphasis on strategic information systems as a result of the changing competitive environment, IT and IS were developed to support business strategic initiatives. The commercialization of the Internet in the mid-1990s created an explosive growth of the Internet and Internet-based business applications. Using the Internet standards, corporations were converting their old incompatible internal networks to intranets, similarly, extranets are being built to link companies with their customers, suppliers, and other business partners.

IT and IS have made it possible to access vast amounts of information easily and quickly. Systems such as enterprise resource planning (ERP) give managers the ability to monitor the operation of the entire organization in real time. Executive information portals have allowed senior managers to take a much more comprehensive view of strategic management than previously. Tools such as the balanced scorecard give a holistic view of business performance by integrating factors in multiple business functions.

In the last few years, business process management (BPM) software has been designed with the aim of closing gaps in the existing ERP deployments. As companies are increasingly faced with problems associated with incompatible functional systems from different vendors, enterprise application integration (EAI) has become an important area. BPM systems have been deployed to lower the cost and complexity of application and data integration. Another recent development is Web Services enabled by standards-based protocols (such as XML, SOAP, UDDI, and WSDL). The wide acceptance of Internet protocols also has also led to the emergence of service-oriented architectures (SOA). SOA focus on building robust and flexible systems that provide services as required in a dynamic business process environment. Instead of being programmed in advance, services are invoked, generated, brokered, and delivered on the fly.

2.2.3 Alignment of IT/IS with Business Strategy

IT/IS in business has evolved and become increasingly integrated with business organizations. Strategic management now encompasses corporate strategy, functional business strategy, information strategy, and IT/IS strategy. For most businesses, their strategies form a multilevel hierarchy. At the very top is corporate strategy, which sets the direction for corporate-level decision-making. Below corporate strategy, there are functional strategies, business unit strategies, and operational strategies. Building a comprehensive strategic IT/IS plan that aligns with the business strategy is essential to ensuring the success of the organization.

Henderson and Venkatraman (1993) introduced *business-IT alignment* intended to support the integration of IT into business strategy. They distinguish in their classic "strategic alignment model" between the business domain (consisting of "business strategy" and "business processes") and the technology domain (consisting of "IT strategy" and "IT processes," including systems development and maintenance) in an organization. Figure 2.1 shows the schematic of the strategic alignment model.

Henderson and Venkatraman described four types of alignment:

1. *Strategic execution:* Business strategy drives organizational infrastructure and processes, ultimately influencing IS infrastructure and processes.
2. *Technology transformation:* Business strategy drives IT strategy, ultimately influencing IT processes.
3. *Competitive potential:* Information strategy influences business strategy, ultimately influencing organizational infrastructure and processes.
4. *Service level:* Information strategy influences IT infrastructure and processes, ultimately influencing organizational infrastructure and processes.

Perspectives on strategic alignment are shown in Figure 2.2.

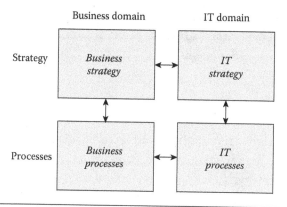

Figure 2.1   Strategic alignment model.

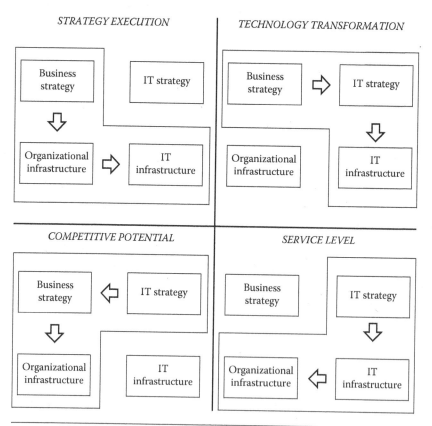

Figure 2.2   Perspectives on strategic alignment.

IT/IS alignment with business strategy is vital to achieve expected results. IT/IS alignment with business strategy can improve business performance. Measuring the degree of IT alignment has been difficult for many businesses. An IT/IS and business strategy alignment maturity model on the lines of the five-level capacity maturity model (CMM) for software engineering can be proposed:

- At the base level, called Nonexistent, there is IT alignment with business strategy. IT plays only a supportive role in operations.
- At the Ad hoc level, the need for IT alignment is recognized, but a systematic approach is lacking. IT supports business goals on a case-by-case basis. There is no attempt to measure the success of IT alignment.
- At the Repeatable level, IT alignment is considered at the enterprise level. However, it is only implemented in some business units. Limited measures of IT alignment exist.
- At the Defined process level, IT alignment is systematically implemented throughout the enterprise, with appropriate policies and procedures to monitor and measure the benefits of the IT alignment.
- At the Optimized level, IT strategy is seamlessly aligned with business strategy at all managerial levels and in all business units. IT alignment processes have been extended to external best practices with other organizations. Measures of IT alignment and feedback mechanisms exist to ensure that IT alignment stays at this level.

Obviously, IT alignment is one of the key issues in strategic management. However, IT alignment is more than simply formulating IT strategy to fit the business strategy. Business strategy is future oriented and subject to external forces and environmental uncertainty. IT alignment should build adaptability into IT strategy. Furthermore, for some technology companies, IT may be the driver of corporate strategy. Strategic management is concerned with the long-term survival and prosperity of organizations. As the environment changes, organizations must also adapt to maintain their viability. Organizations evolve, and so do strategies. Thus, strategic management is also a learning process. There are four basic learning behaviors in strategy formulation, namely natural selection, imitation, reinforcement, and best reply. In each of the four learning processes, IT and IS are becoming indispensable:

- Natural selection stipulates that organizations that use high-payoff strategies have competitive advantages over those using low-payoff strategies. As a result, high-payoff strategies have a better chance to be continued by surviving organizations. Determining the payoff of strategies, thus, is very important in this kind of strategic learning behavior.
- Imitation describes how organizations mimic the practices of successful peers in their industry. This is the cause of herding behavior in which the outcome is not clear, but organizations jump on the bandwagon, simply following what many of their peers are doing. A classic example was the dotcom bubble during the late 1990s.
- Reinforcement is concerned with how organizations monitor their own behaviors and favor the strategies that resulted in high payoffs in the past. In contrast to natural selection, reinforcement learning is based on one's own experience rather than others' experience.
- Best reply is the behavior wherein organizations formulate their strategies based on what they expect their competitors will do. Many of the popular competitive strategies, such as low-cost leadership and differentiation, fall into this category.

2.3 Summary

IT alignment is one of the key issues in strategic management. However, IT alignment is more than simply formulating IT strategy to fit the business strategy. Business strategy is future-oriented and subject to external forces and environmental uncertainty. IT alignment should build adaptability into IT strategy. Furthermore, for some technology companies, IT may be the driver of corporate strategy.

PART I
GENESIS OF PERFORMANCE INTELLIGENCE

3

DECISION SUPPORT SYSTEMS

This chapter introduces the nature, type, and scope of decisions. It discusses the decision-making process and the techniques used for making decisions. Five broad DSS categories are explained including data-driven, model-driven, communications-driven, document-driven, knowledge-driven, and decision support systems (DSS). The latter half of the chapter presents a generic DSS architecture to enable discussion of text, hypertext, database, spreadsheet, rule-oriented, and compound DSS.

3.1 Decisions

A decision is a choice from multiple alternatives, usually made with a fair degree of rationality. In an enterprise, these decisions may concern the development of a strategic plan and imply therefore substantial investment choices, the definition of marketing initiatives and related sales predictions, and the design of a production plan that allows the available human and technological resources to be employed in an effective and efficient way.

The decision-making process is part of a broader subject usually referred to as problem solving, which refers to the process through which individuals try to bridge the gap between the current operating conditions of a system (as is) and the supposedly better conditions to be achieved in the future (to be). In general, the transition of a system toward the desired state implies overcoming certain obstacles and is not easy to attain. This forces decision makers to devise a set of alternative feasible options to achieve the desired goal, and then choose a decision based on a comparison between the advantages and disadvantages of each option. Hence, the decision selected must be put into practice and then verified to determine if it has enabled the planned objectives to be achieved. When this fails to happen, the problem is reconsidered, according to a recursive logic.

Management decisions differ depending on the level of responsibility on which they are made and who makes them. A brief overview is helpful here to put this into context:

1. Strategic decisions have significant resource allocation impact, set the precedents or tone for decisions further down the organization, and have a potentially material effect on the organization's competitiveness within its marketplace. They are made by top managers and affect the business direction of an organization.

   Strategic intelligence is arguably the most vital form of intelligence because it provides a framework within which other forms of intelligence collection and analysis take place. It helps to discern and make sense of important trends, to identify and extract patterns that would otherwise not be visible, and to provide an overall picture of the evolving opportunity and threat environment. Strategic intelligence also provides guidance for tactical and operational assessments, and work done at these levels, in turn, helps to shape the strategic intelligence focus. As strategic analytic methodologies mature, they will also offer the basis for predictive or anticipatory assessments that can serve to provide warning of potential high-impact activities.

   Generic strategic analytical methodologies are as follows:
   - *Sector/competitor assessments* focus on emerging or threatening competitors that provide strong potential for impacting the competitive terrain.
   - *Pattern or trend analyses* are baseline assessments to better recognize deviations from current practice, especially those that shape the industry's future.
   - *Anti-pattern or anomaly detection* requires systematic "environmental scanning," as well as the collating of tactical and operational intelligence reports that identify and highlight specific deviations from the norm.
   - *Opportunity and threat (O&T) assessments* are used to assess the levels of dependence and vulnerabilities of

critical issues, competitive changes that could cause significant impact, and the likelihood of such activities taking place.

- *Impact assessments* include the macrolevel view taken in strategic intelligence analysis (SIA) which offers a good approach for assessing probable cascade effects of threatening competitive action and activity.

2. Tactical decisions are less pervasive than strategic ones and involve formulating and implementing policies for the organization. They are usually made by mid-level managers and often materially affect functions such as marketing, accounting, production, a business unit, or product, as opposed to the entire organization. Tactical decisions generally have lower resource implications than strategic decisions and are typically semistructured.

Tactical intelligence analysis (TIA) is a necessary and important complement to work done at the strategic level. It is the natural link between macro- and microlevel analyses. Although SIA provides the framework for TIA, these assessments, in turn, feed SIA. With a dynamic symbiotic relationship between the two, mutual strength is derived.

Generic tactical analytical initiatives are as follows:

- *Cluster and pattern analysis* identifies the use of particular marketplace attack methods, commonalities of targets, and attempts to build profiles of competitors.
- *Value constellation analysis* identifies the key stakeholders, important partners, allies, joint venture prospects, outsourcing potential, and agents that a company could utilize.
- *Stimulus–response analysis* identifies actions that could be taken by competitors in response to specific events. This analysis could be used both proactively to develop warnings and reactively to design future tactics.

3. Operational decisions support the day-to-day decisions needed to operate the organization and take effect for a few days or weeks. Typically made by a lower level manager, operational decisions are distinct from tactical and strategic decisions in that they are made frequently and often "on the sly."

Operational decisions tend to be highly structured, often with well-defined procedure manuals.

Operational intelligence analysis is often event-centric and single-case-oriented. It provides more immediate but lesser lasting benefits and typically involves technological assessments of methods used for marketplace battles or investigations of competitive threats.

Generic operational analytical initiatives are as follows:

- *Competitor analysis* helps in planning and executing competitive intelligence efforts at appropriate time and preventing premature disclosures.
- *Vulnerability analysis* helps in identifying marketplace vulnerabilities and measures that can rectify, minimize, or eliminate them.

3.1.1 Types of Decisions

Organizational decision problems are of various types, from daily operational decisions to long-term strategy business decisions, from internal single decisions to multilevel decisions or multi-organizational decisions. Decision makers can be at various levels according to their decision problems, such as product distributors, supermarket managers, or heads of department. Organizational decision-making seeks to find the optimal or most satisfactory solution for a decision problem such as selecting the best from a set of product prototypes, making an optimized resource plan, choosing the most suitable supplier and determining a product's price. Different decision-making tasks may have different features and therefore are modeled in different forms or presented by different methods, and solved by different decision support techniques.

A classical classification is based on a given problem's degree of complexity:

1. *Structured*: A structured decision problem can be described by classic mathematical models, such as linear programming or statistical methods. A typical structured decision example is the selection of a supplier who has the lowest price of all the suppliers with the same quality/type of products, or determination of a product plan which will bring the highest profit

of all the possible product plans in a factory. The procedures for obtaining optimal solutions are known as standard solution methods. For example, goal programming can be used to solve a linear programming model when the decision maker provides a goal for their decision objective.

2. *Semi-structured*: Semi-structured decision problems fall between structured and unstructured problems, having both structured and unstructured features, and reflecting most real-world situations. Solving semi-structured decision problems involves a combination of both standard optimization solution procedures and human judgment, and also needs the support of related intelligent information processing techniques and inference approaches.

3. *Unstructured*: An unstructured decision problem is fuzzy, uncertain and vague, for which there is no standard solution method for obtaining an optimal solution, or where such an optimal solution does not exist. Human intuition is often the basis for decision-making in an unstructured problem. Typical unstructured problems include planning new services for customers, hiring an executive for a big company, choosing a set of development projects for a long period, or deciding on a set of policies for a social issue.

Multilevel decision-making (MLDM) problems arise in many situations which require compromise between the objectives of two or more interacting entities and these entities are arranged within a hierarchical structure with independent and perhaps conflicting objectives.

Computer-based decision support techniques can be more useful in structured and semi-structured decision problems than unstructured decision problems. In an unstructured decision problem, only part of the problem can be assisted by computerized decision support techniques. For semi-structured decision problems, a computerized decision support technique can improve the quality of the information on which a decision is based, therefore increasing the decision maker's situation awareness to reach a better decision and improve decision efficiency.

3.1.2 Scope of Decisions

1. *Strategic decisions*: Decisions are strategic when they affect the entire organization or at least a substantial part of it for a long period of time. Strategic decisions strongly influence the general objectives and policies of an enterprise. As a consequence, strategic decisions are taken at a higher organizational level, usually by the company top management.

2. *Managerial decisions*: Tactical decisions affect only parts of an enterprise and are usually restricted to a single department. The time span is limited to a medium-term horizon, typically up to a year. Tactical decisions place themselves within the context determined by strategic decisions. In a company hierarchy, tactical decisions are made by middle managers, such as the heads of company departments.

3. *Operational decisions*: Operational decisions refer to specific activities carried out within an organization and have a modest impact on the future. Operational decisions are framed within the elements and conditions determined by strategic and tactical decisions. Therefore, they are usually made at a lower organizational level, by knowledge workers responsible for a single activity or task such as subdepartment heads, workshop foremen, and back-office heads.

The characteristics of the intelligence required in a decision-making process will change depending on the scope of the decisions to be supported (see Figure 3.1).

3.2 Decision-Making Process

The nature of a decision process depends on many factors, such as the characteristics of the organization within which the system is placed, the subjective attitudes of the decision makers, the availability of appropriate problem-solving methodologies, and the availability of effective decision support tools.

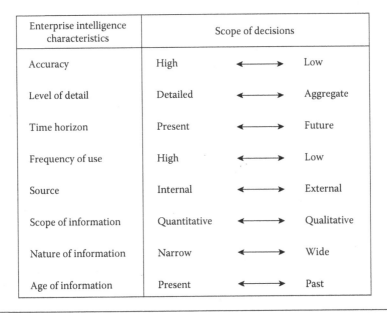

Enterprise intelligence characteristics	Scope of decisions		
Accuracy	High	←→	Low
Level of detail	Detailed	←→	Aggregate
Time horizon	Present	←→	Future
Frequency of use	High	←→	Low
Source	Internal	←→	External
Scope of information	Quantitative	←→	Qualitative
Nature of information	Narrow	←→	Wide
Age of information	Present	←→	Past

Figure 3.1 The characteristics of enterprise intelligence in terms of the scope of the decisions.

The decision-making process has the following characteristics:

- The decisions made within a public or private enterprise or organization are often interconnected and determine broad effects. Each decision has consequences for many individuals and several parts of the organization.
- Decisions are often devised by a group of individuals instead of a single decision maker.
- The number of alternative actions may be very high, and sometimes unlimited.
- The effects of a given decision usually appear later, not immediately.
- Experiments carried out in a real-world system, according to a trial-and-error scheme, are too costly and risky to be of practical use for decision-making.
- The dynamics in which an enterprise operates is strongly affected by the pressure of a competitive environment, which implies that knowledge workers need to address situations and make decisions quickly and in a timely fashion.

- During the decision-making process, knowledge workers are asked to access data and information, and work on them based on a conceptual and analytical framework.
- Feedback plays an important role in providing information and knowledge for future decision-making processes within a given organization.
- In most instances, the decision-making process has multiple goals, with different performance indicators, that might be in conflict with one another.
- Many decisions are made in a fuzzy context and entail risk factors. The level of propensity or aversion to risk varies significantly among different individuals.

Decision-making processes consists of following steps:

1. *Intelligence*: In the intelligence phase the task of the decision maker is to identify, circumscribe, and explicitly define the problem that emerges in the system under study. Analysis of the context and all the available information may allow decision makers to quickly understand the signals and symptoms indicating a corrective action to improve system performance. For example, during the execution of a project, the intelligence phase may consist of a comparison between the current progress of the activities and the original development plan. In general, it is important not to confuse the problem with the symptoms. For example, suppose that an e-commerce bookseller receives a complaint concerning late delivery of a book order placed online. Such inconvenience may be interpreted as the problem and be tackled by arranging a second delivery by priority shipping to circumvent the dissatisfaction of the customer.

2. *Design*: In the design phase actions aimed at solving the identified problem should be developed and planned. At this level, the experience and creativity of the decision makers play a critical role, as they are asked to devise viable solutions that ultimately allow the intended purpose to be achieved. Where the number of available actions is small, decision makers can make an explicit enumeration of the alternatives to identify the best solution. If, on the other hand, the number of alternatives is very large, or even unlimited, their identification occurs in

an implicit way, usually through a description of the rules that feasible actions should satisfy. For example, these rules may directly translate into the constraints of an optimization model.

3. *Choice*: Once the alternative actions have been identified, it is necessary to evaluate them on the basis of the performance criteria deemed significant. Mathematical models and the corresponding solution methods usually play a valuable role during the choice phase. For example, optimization models and methods allow the best solution to be found in very complex situations involving countless or even infinite feasible solutions. On the other hand, decision trees can be used to handle decision-making processes influenced by stochastic events.

4. *Implementation*: When the best alternative has been selected by the decision maker, it is transformed into actions by means of an implementation plan. This involves assigning responsibilities and roles to all those involved in the action plan.

5. *Control*: Once the action has been implemented, it is then necessary to verify and check that the original expectations have been satisfied and the effects of the action match the original intentions. In particular, the differences between the values of the performance indicators identified in the choice phase and the values actually observed at the end of the implementation plan should be measured. In an adequately planned DSS, the results of these evaluations translate into experience and information, which are then transferred into the data warehouse to be used during subsequent decision-making processes.

3.3 Decision-Making Techniques

Decision techniques involved in modeling and executing the decision-making process are as follows.

3.3.1 Mathematical Programming

Mathematical programming or optimization refers to the study of decision-making problems in which one seeks to minimize or maximize a function by systematically choosing the values of variables from an allowed set (a feasible set). A mathematical programming model includes three sets of elements: decision variables, objective functions, and constraints (constraint conditions), where uncontrollable variables or parameters are within the objective functions and the constraints. Many real-world decision problems can be modeled by mathematical programming models.

Different types of mathematical programming models are:

- Linear programming
- Multi-objective programming
- Bi-level/multilevel programming

Linear programming is an important type of mathematical optimization in which there is only one objective function, and the objective function and constraints are expressions of linear relationships among decision variables. Linear programming is heavily used in various management activities, either to maximize the profit or minimize the cost of an organization.

3.3.2 Multi-Criteria Decision-Making

When we need to select the best option from a list of alternatives based on multiple criteria for a decision problem, it is often necessary to analyze each alternative in the light of its determination of each of these criteria. Multi-criteria decision-making (MCDM), also called multi-attribute decision-making (MADM), refers to making preferred decisions (e.g., evaluation, prioritization, and selection) in the presence of multiple and conflicting criteria over the alternatives available. An MCDM utility model combines all the criteria of a given alternative simultaneously through the use of a specific utility formula or utility function. Problems for MCDM may range from those in our daily life, such as the selection of a restaurant, to those affecting entire nations.

3.3.3 Case-Based Reasoning

Many decision problems cannot be modeled by mathematical programming models. Managers often produce a solution for a given problem based on their previous experience and knowledge. Case-based reasoning (CBR) provides an effective methodology for DSS in solving a new problem based on the solutions of similar past problems.

The technique of CBR provides a powerful learning ability which uses past experiences as a basis for dealing with new similar problems. A CBR system can, therefore, facilitate the knowledge acquisition process by eliminating the time required to elicit solutions from experts. In dynamically changing situations where the problem cannot be modeled by mathematical models and solutions are not easy to generate, CBR is the preferred method of reasoning.

3.3.4 Data Warehouse and Data Mining

A data warehouse is a repository of an organization's electronically stored data. A data warehouse system involves not only data storage but also the techniques to retrieve and analyze data, to extract, transform and load data, and to manage the data dictionary. In particular, the data warehouse includes business intelligence tools to implement the above functions to better support business decision-making.

Data mining is the process of extracting hidden and undiscovered patterns from data and is commonly used in a wide range of profiling practices and knowledge discovery projects. Rules and patterns are discovered from data with the aim of identifying a set of options or decisions. In most data mining applications, a data file of query results is created from a data warehouse and then analyzed by a specialist using artificial intelligence or statistical tools.

3.3.5 Decision Tree

A decision tree is a graphic representation of a set of decision rules and their possible consequences. It can be used to create a plan to reach the goal of a decision. A decision tree, as a special form of tree structure, is a predictive model to map observations about an item with conclusions about the item's target value. Each interior node corresponds to a variable and an arc to a child node represents a possible value or splitting condition of that variable. The decision tree approach, as a decision support tool, models a decision problem and its possible consequences in a tree-like graph. It is very suitable for a decision which involves possible chance event outcomes, resource costs, and utility. Decision trees are commonly used in decision analysis to help identify the strategy which is most likely to reach a goal. In applications, a decision tree or consequences can contain fuzzy numbers or linguistic terms and are therefore called fuzzy decision trees.

3.3.6 Fuzzy Sets and Systems

Whatever decision techniques are used, a critical issue to deal with is uncertainty. Decision environments and data sources often have various uncertain factors, resulting in uncertain relations among decision objectives and decision entities. For example, an individual's preference for alternatives and judgment for criteria are often expressed by linguistic terms, such as "low" and "high," which are uncertain expressions. Precise mathematical and inference approaches are not efficient enough to tackle such uncertainty.

Various uncertain information processing techniques have therefore been developed by using fuzzy sets, fuzzy numbers, and fuzzy logic in decision-making activities. Research results include new methodologies and algorithms for fuzzy multi-objective decision-making, fuzzy multi-criteria decision-making, fuzzy case-based reasoning, fuzzy decision trees, fuzzy data retrieval, and fuzzy association rules. Various applications of fuzzy decision-making have been developed as well.

3.4 Decision Support Systems

Decision support systems (DSS) enable decisions based on the data collected through the various systems across the enterprise.

3.4.1 Multi-Source Driven DSS

1. *Data-Driven DSS*: Data-driven DSS emphasize access to and manipulation of a time series of internal company data and sometimes external and real-time data. Simple file systems accessed by query and retrieval tools provide the most elementary level of functionality. Data warehouse systems that allow the manipulation of data by computerized tools tailored to a specific task and setting or by more general tools and operators provide additional functionality. Data-driven DSS with online analytical processing provide the highest level of

functionality and decision support that is linked to analysis of large collections of historical data.

2. *Model-Driven DSS*: Model-driven DSS emphasize access to and manipulation of financial, optimization, and/or simulation models. Simple quantitative models provide the most elementary level of functionality. Model-driven DSS use limited data and parameters provided by decision makers to aid decision makers in analyzing a situation, but in general large data bases are not needed for model-driven DSS. In 1978, Dan Bricklin and Bob Frankston co-wrote the software program VisiCalc (visible calculator). VisiCalc provided managers with the opportunity for hands-on computer-based analysis and decision support at a reasonably low cost. VisiCalc was the first "killer" application for personal computers and made possible the development of many model-oriented, personal DSS for use by managers.

3. *Communication-driven DSS*: Communications-driven DSS use network and communications technologies to facilitate decision-relevant collaboration and communication. In these systems, communication technologies are the dominant architectural component. Tools used include groupware, video conferencing, and computer-based bulletin boards. D. Engelbart's 1962 paper "Augmenting human intellect: a conceptual framework" is the anchor for much of the later work related to communications-driven DSS. In 1989, Lotus introduced a groupware product called Notes and broadened the focus of group DSS (GDSS) to include enhanced communication, collaboration, and coordination among groups of people. Notes had its roots in a product called PLATO Notes, written at the Computer-based Education Research Laboratory (CERL) at the University of Illinois in 1973 by David R. Woolley.

In general, groupware, bulletin boards, audio and video-conferencing are the primary technologies for communications-driven decision support. In the past few years, voice and video delivered using the Internet protocol have greatly expanded the possibilities for synchronous communications-driven DSS.

4. *Knowledge-driven DSS*: Knowledge-driven DSS can suggest or recommend actions to managers. These DSS are

person–computer systems with specialized problem-solving expertise. The expertise consists of knowledge about a particular domain, understanding of problems within that domain, and skill at solving some of these problems. In 1965, a Stanford University research team led by Edward Feigenbaum created the DENDRAL expert system. DENDRAL led to the development of other rule-based reasoning programs including MYCIN, which helped physicians diagnose blood diseases based on sets of clinical symptoms. The MYCIN project resulted in the development of the first expert-system shell. In 1983, Dustin Huntington established EXSYS. That company and its products made it practical to use PC-based tools to develop expert systems.

Artificial intelligence (AI) systems have been developed to detect fraud and expedite financial transactions, many additional medical diagnostic systems have been based on AI, and expert systems have been used for scheduling in manufacturing operation and web-based advisory systems. In recent years, connecting expert systems technologies to relational databases with web-based front ends has broadened the deployment and use of knowledge-driven DSS.

5. *Document-Driven DSS*: A document-driven DSS uses computer storage and processing technologies to provide document retrieval and analysis. Large document databases may include scanned documents, hypertext documents, images, sounds, and video. Examples of documents that might be accessed by a document-driven DSS are policies and procedures, product specifications, catalogs, and corporate historical documents, including minutes of meetings and correspondence. A search engine is a primary decision-aiding tool associated with a document-driven DSS. These systems have also been called text-oriented DSS. The precursor for this type of DSS is Vannevar Bush's (1945) article titled "As we may think." Bush wrote: "Consider a future device for individual use, which is a sort of mechanized private file and library. It needs a name, and to coin one at random, 'memex' will do." Bush's memex is a much broader vision than that of today's document-driven DSS.

By 1995, T. Berners-Lee's world-wide web was recognized by a number of software developers and academics as a serious platform for implementing all types of DSS.

Beginning in approximately 1995, the world-wide web and global internet provided a technology platform for further extending the capabilities and deployment of computerized decision support. The release of the HTML 2.0 specifications with form tags and tables was a turning point in the development of web-based DSS. New handheld PCs, wireless networks, expanding parallel processing coupled with very large databases, and visualization tools are continuing to encourage the development of innovative decision support applications.

3.4.2 Generic DSS Architecture

DSS are defined in terms of the roles they play in decision processes; they enhance the processes and/or outcomes of decision-making. They provide knowledge and/or knowledge-processing capability that is instrumental in making decisions or making sense of decision situations.

Generic architecture furnishes a unifying framework for guiding explorations of the multitude of issues related to designing, using, and evaluating these systems. The general architecture of houses identifies such important elements as a plumbing system, an electrical system, an air-treatment system, and a system of rooms. It also identifies relationships among these elements. Similarly, the architecture of DSS can be described by a generic framework that identifies essential elements of a DSS and their interrelationships.

Structurally, a DSS has four essential components:

1. A language system (LS) consisting of all messages the DSS can accept
2. A presentation system (PS) consisting of all messages the DSS can emit
3. A knowledge system (KS) consisting of all knowledge the DSS has stored and retained
4. A problem-processing system (PPS) which tries to recognize and solve problems (i.e., process problems) during the making of a decision

The architecture emphasizes the importance of knowledge representation and processing in the functioning of a DSS and advanced the idea of a generalized problem-processing system. This is a PPS that is invariant across a large array of DSS and decision-making applications, with all variations being accommodated by different KS that all work with the same PPS.

Even though a relatively generalized problem processor can exist, DSS can also differ by having diverse PPS. All PPS possess the first-order abilities of acquisition, selection, assimilation, and emission. Many have a knowledge-generation ability too. The exact character of each ability can differ widely from one problem-processing system to the next. When a PPS employs a spreadsheet-processing approach, the DSS knowledge system uses a corresponding spreadsheet approach to knowledge representation. In contrast, if a DSS problem processor relies on a database-management technique for processing knowledge, then its KS must contain knowledge represented in terms of databases. In other words, DSS can differ with respect to the knowledge-management techniques with which their PPS are equipped and that govern the usable representations held in their KS.

Many special cases of the generic DSS architecture can be identified by viewing KS contents and PPS abilities in terms of the knowledge-management techniques employed by a DSS:

1. *Text-oriented DSS*: In the 1970s and especially in the 1980s, text management emerged as an important, widely used computerized means for representing and processing pieces of text. The LS contains requests corresponding to the various allowed manipulations. It may also contain requests that let a user ask for assistance covering some aspect of the DSS. The PS consists of images of stored text that can be emitted, plus messages that can help the decision maker use the DSS. The PPS consists of software that can perform various manipulations on contents of any of the stored documents. It may also involve software that can help a user in making requests.

   A text-oriented DSS supports a decision maker by electronically keeping track of textually represented knowledge that could have a bearing on decisions. It allows documents to be electronically created, revised, and reviewed by a decision maker on an as-needed basis. The viewing can be exploratory browsing in search of stimulation or a focused search for some particular piece of knowledge needed in to make a decision.

However, there is a problem with traditional text management: it is not convenient to trace a flow of ideas through separate pieces of text. There is no explicit relationship or connection between the knowledge held in one text file and the knowledge in another.

2. *Hypertext-oriented DSS*: This problem is remedied by a technique known as hypertext. Each piece of text is linked to other pieces of text that are conceptually related to it. In addition to the PPS capabilities of a traditional text-oriented DSS, a user can request the creation, deletion, and traversal of links. In traversing a link, the PPS shifts its focus (and the user's) from one piece of text to another. This ad hoc traversal through associated pieces of textcontinues at your discretion, resembling a flow of thoughts through the many associated concepts in your own mind.

The benefit of this hypertext kind of DSS is that it supplements a decision maker's own capabilities by accurately storing and recalling large volumes of concepts and connections that he or she is not inclined personally to memorize.

Web-oriented DSS comprise a large portion of hypertext-oriented DSS.

3. *Database-oriented DSS*: The knowledge handled by database-oriented DSS tends to be primarily descriptive, rigidly structured, and often extremely voluminous. Like text-oriented DSS, these systems aid decision makers by accurately tracking and selectively recalling knowledge that satisfies a particular need or serves to stimulate ideas. Rather than treating data as streams of text, they are organized in a highly structured, tabular fashion. The processing of these data tables is designed to take advantage of their high degree of structure.

The PPS has three kinds of software: a database control system, an interactive query processing system, and various custom-built processing systems. One, but not both, of the latter two could be omitted from the DSS. The database control system consists of capabilities for manipulating table structures and contents (e.g., defining or revising table structures, finding or updating records, creating or deleting records, and building new tables from existing ones). These capabilities are used by the query processor and custom-built processors in their efforts at satisfying user requests.

For a variety of reasons, rather than dealing with the standard query processors, users may prefer to deal with custom-built processors or application programs because:

- They may give responses more quickly to requests a standard query could not handle, presenting responses in a specially tailored fashion without requiring the user to learn the syntax of a query language or to use as many keystrokes.
- They may provide the logic to interpret some custom-designed set of requests.
- They may give commands to the database control system, telling it what database manipulations to perform for each possible request.
- They may also supply the logic necessary for packaging responses in a customized manner.
- They may even perform some calculation(s) to generate new knowledge based on values from the database. Calculation results can be included in an emitted response and/or assimilated into the KS for subsequent use.

By the 1990s, a special class of database systems known as data warehouses had emerged. A data warehouse is a large collection of data integrated from multiple operational systems, oriented toward a particular subject domain, whose content is not over-written or discarded, but is time-stamped as it is assimilated. A data warehouse may have the look of a relational database or a multidimensional database. Data warehouse technology was specifically conceived to devise KS for high-performance support of decision-making processes.

In the case of a database-oriented DSS, extensive procedural knowledge cannot be readily represented in the KS. However, the application programs that form part of the PPS can contain instructions for analyzing data selected from the database. By carrying out these procedures, the PPS can emit new knowledge (e.g., a sales forecast) that has been generated from KS contents (e.g., records of past sales trends). But, because they are part of the PPS, a user cannot readily view, modify or create such procedures, as can be done in the text-oriented case.

4. *Spreadsheet-oriented DSS*: Using the spreadsheet technique for knowledge management, a DSS user can not only create, view, and modify procedural knowledge assimilated in the KS, but can also tell the PPS to carry out the instructions they contain. This gives DSS users much more power in handling procedural knowledge than is achievable with either text management or database management. In addition, spreadsheet management is able to deal with descriptive knowledge.

However, it is not nearly as convenient as database management in handling large volumes of descriptive knowledge, nor does it allow a user to readily represent and process data in textual passages.

Spreadsheet-oriented DSS are typically used for what-if analyses in order to see the implications of some set of assumptions embodied in the cell definitions. They support a decision maker by giving a rapid means of revaluating various alternatives.

5. *Rule-oriented DSS*: DSS architecture is based on a knowledge management technique that involves representing and processing rules. This technique evolved within the field of artificial intelligence, giving computers the ability to manage reasoning knowledge. Recall that reasoning knowledge tells us what conclusions are valid when a certain situation exists. Rules offer a straightforward, convenient means for

representing such fragments of knowledge. A rule has the basic form of:

If: description of a possible situation (premise)

Then: indication of actions to take (conclusion)

Because: justification for taking those actions (reason)

This format says that if the possible situation can be determined to exist, then the indicated actions should be carried out for the reasons given. In other words, if the premise is true, then the conclusion is valid.

The KS of a rule-oriented DSS holds one or more rule sets, where each rule set pertains to reasoning about what recommendation to give a user seeking advice on some subject. Additionally, a KS can contain descriptions of the current state of affairs (e.g., current machine settings, locations of competing outlets, an investor's present financial situation). Such state descriptions can be thought of as values that have been assigned to variables.

Aside from requests for help and for editing state descriptions, users of a rule-oriented DSS can issue various types of requests for decision support purposes:

a. The LS can contain requests for advice and requests for explanation.

b. The problem processor for a rule-oriented DSS has capabilities for creating, revising, and deleting state descriptions. Of greater interest is the capability to do logical inference (i.e., to reason) with a set of rules to produce advice sought by a user. The problem processor examines pertinent rules in a rule set, looking for those whose premises are true for the present situation. This situation is defined by current state descriptions (e.g., machine settings) and the user's request for advice (e.g., citing the nature of the quality defect). When the PPS finds a true premise, it takes the actions specified in that rule's conclusion. This action sheds further light on the situation, which allows premises of still other rules to be established as true, causing actions indicated in their conclusions to be taken. Reasoning continues in this way until some action is taken that yields the requested advice or the PPS gives up due to insufficient knowledge in its KS. The PPS also has the ability to explain its behavior both during and after conducting the inference. There are many possible variations for the inference process for both the forward reasoning approach just outlined and the alternative reverse-reasoning approach which involves goal seeking.

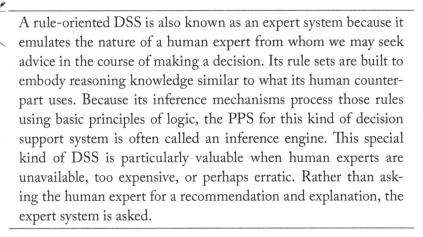

A rule-oriented DSS is also known as an expert system because it emulates the nature of a human expert from whom we may seek advice in the course of making a decision. Its rule sets are built to embody reasoning knowledge similar to what its human counterpart uses. Because its inference mechanisms process those rules using basic principles of logic, the PPS for this kind of decision support system is often called an inference engine. This special kind of DSS is particularly valuable when human experts are unavailable, too expensive, or perhaps erratic. Rather than asking the human expert for a recommendation and explanation, the expert system is asked.

6. *Compound DSS*: Each generic DSS framework tends to emphasize one knowledge-management technique; however, if a decision maker would like the kinds of support offered by multiple knowledge management techniques, either one can use multiple DSS, each oriented toward a particular technique, or one can use a single DSS that encompasses multiple techniques. The first option is akin to having multiple staff assistants, each of whom is well versed in a single knowledge-management technique. When results of using one technique need to be processed via another technique, it is the decision maker's responsibility to translate responses from one DSS into requests to another DSS. The second option is akin to having a staff assistant who is adept at multiple knowledge-management techniques. There is one LS and one PS for the decision maker to learn. Although they are probably more extensive than those of a particular single-technique DSS, they are likely less demanding than coping with the sum total of LS and PS for all corresponding single-technique DSS.

The effort required of a decision maker who wants to use the results of one technique in the processing of another technique varies, depending on the way in which the multiple techniques have been integrated into a single compound DSS.

3.5 Summary

This chapter has introduced the generic DSS architecture. From the perspective of this framework, a DSS can be studied in terms of four interrelated elements: a language system, a presentation system, a knowledge system, and a problem-processing system. The first three of these are systems of representation: the set of all requests a user can make, the set of all responses the DSS can present, and the knowledge representations presently stored in the DSS. The problem processor is a dynamic system that can accept any request in the LS and react with a corresponding response from the PS. Each special case of the generic DSS architecture characterizes a distinct class of DSS including text, hypertext, database, spreadsheet, rule, and compound DSS.

PART II
ROAD TO PERFORMANCE INTELLIGENCE

4

DATABASE SYSTEMS

The genesis of big data computing can be traced to the development of databases in the 1960s. For most of computing history, database solutions have been focused on capturing, storing, managing, querying, and analyzing structured data. The advent of the Internet and the emergence of end-consumer solutions, su web portals, social networks, and mobility solutions, have resulted in a deluge of unstructured and real-time data that have to be mined in order to detect patterns of significance critical for the functioning of the digital economy. But the journey commenced with traditional databases (hierarchical, network, and relational), which evolved into more refined object-oriented databases. This chapter presents an overview of the characteristics of these traditional databases and lessons learnt from using, developing, and maintaining them.

4.1 Database Management System

A database management system (DBMS) provides the needed organizational approach to flexible storage and retrieval of large amounts of data. A DBMS provides for the organization of the data elements, the representation of relationships among the elements, and a uniform interface for users. A database is a self-describing collection of data elements and their relationships, which presents a uniform interface to users. A DBMS supports the reliable storage of the database, implements the relationship structures, and offers uniform storage/retrieval services to users.

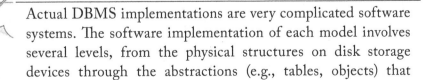

Actual DBMS implementations are very complicated software systems. The software implementation of each model involves several levels, from the physical structures on disk storage devices through the abstractions (e.g., tables, objects) that describe an application. Variations occur both in the expression of the model structures and in the extra features that distinguish a product from its competitors.

A database is a self-describing collection of data elements, together with relationships among those elements, that presents a uniform service interface. A database management system (DBMS) is a software product that supports the reliable storage of the database, implements the structures for maintaining relationships and constraints, and offers storage and retrieval services to users. Additional features address other issues, such as simultaneous access, security, backup, and recovery. This implies that the data elements reside in a self-describing structure, like a table, which confers meaning on them. A database system isolates the computer-related problems of large-volume data storage and retrieval from application-oriented issues. It simplifies software development efforts by providing generic services adaptable to varying applications. It also contributes to the efficiency of many interfacing programs dealing with the same data environment by providing self-describing, consistent data to all users. Moreover, a database system provides a general approach for maintaining relationships among data elements.

Database users can be individuals dealing with an interactive interface or other computer programs requesting services with calls to sub-procedures provided by the DBMS. Although some differences distinguish these two modes of service, the DBMS should provide as much uniformity as possible to its users. The user interface module of the DBMS responds to service requests, using the data dictionary to confirm the existence and compatibility of data elements mentioned in the requests. A second module processes storage-retrieval requests, performs optimizations necessary to reduce execution time, and carries out the data operations needed to respond. The DBMS passes the requested data items and any error messages back to the interface module for relay to the user.

Separating data storage and retrieval details into a self-sufficient module is sound software engineering practice. Database systems have overcome other deficiencies in the predatabase mode of operation which used individual programs with their own tailored input/output files.

The development of databases helped to avoid the following problems with older systems:

1. Unhealthy dependence between data and programs
2. Repetition of data elements
3. Opportunities for inconsistencies
4. Unorganized scattering of related data across many files
5. Distributed ownership of data
6. Decentralized security
7. Unregulated interactions between programs using the same data
8. Inadequate multiuser access
9. *Ad hoc* approaches to error recovery
10. Overdependence on physical considerations, such as disk track and sector addresses

4.1.1 DBMS Benefits

The deficiencies of predatabase information processing include encoded data, interdependence between programs and data files, data repetition and associated inconsistencies, ad hoc representation of relationships among data items, lack of coordination across programs using common data, restricted simultaneous access to data, and non-uniform error recovery methods.

1. Without databases, data and the programs are heavily dependent on each other. A program requires its input files or data in order to execute. But data are meaningful only in the context of the program; you need the program to understand the data's meaning. Data should not depend on a program to render it understandable and useful, that is, data should be self-describing.
2. Without a central database repository, programs must frequently access data from separate files. A flexible storage and retrieval mechanism should maintain relationships on an equal footing with the individual data elements.
3. In a nondatabase context, each programmer "owns" the data files associated with his program, making these files less accessible to others. By contrast, a database provides more uniform availability of data.

4. Without a centralized database, the security policy must deal with a dispersed collection of files of varying formats. However, the centralized approach has one uncomfortable security disadvantage: if the central facility is compromised, all the data are exposed.

5. Without databases, programs can interfere with one another. The effects of transactions in one program are not isolated from those in other programs.

6. Data deletions or updates can produce inconsistencies, which are difficult to control in a nondatabase system. A database can coordinate deletion activities, ensuring that no dangling references remain after a deletion.

7. Without databases, data sharing is more difficult. A database can coordinate simultaneous access to the data elements. It allows data sharing at a finer resolution, locking only individual data elements during write operations.

8. Without database oversight, data inconsistencies can arise when a long process terminates with an error. The DBMS rejects a transaction that does not complete, with the state of the database remaining as though the transaction had never started. Because the DBMS handles recovery, individual applications need not deal with failed transactions.

9. Without databases, variations in the physical data representation can cause many problems. A database enables programs to be concerned with manipulating the application objects (e.g., persons, tasks, hours, accounts), not with storage details.

4.2 Database Models

A database model is an organizing principle that specifies particular mechanisms for data storage and retrieval. The model explains, in terms of the services available to an interfacing application, how to access a data element when other related data elements are known. It also specifies the precise meaning of the term "related data" and provides mappings from particular relationships in an application to the more generic types maintained by the DBMS. As an illustration, a relationship exists between each room and the building that houses it, or between each fish and the tank that contains it. The DBMS provides a more general type of relationship in which a container object includes component objects. A database model must allow the representation of a specific building-rooms relationship within the more general container-components framework.

A database model is an abstract approach for organizing data elements and their relationships. The relational model is currently the most popular model; the hierarchical and network models represent prerelational technologies, and the object-oriented model represents postrelational technologies.

The four models examined in this text are hierarchical and network (past), relational (present), and object-oriented and deductive (future). The models differ primarily in the way they represent relationships. The hierarchical model uses a tree format to relate application entities. The tree can be expressed as a linear list, and logical proximity in that linear form implies relations among data elements. The network model provides auxiliary structures, best envisioned as intersecting chains. Navigating along these chains recovers related data elements. The relational model uses common attributes between disjoint tables to relate rows. In one table the attribute serves to identify the row in question; in the other table the same attribute serves as an embedded reference back to that row. The object-oriented model uses logical containment. Since object attributes can be other objects, related data elements can be found through a recursive search within the attributes of a given data element. Finally, the deductive model uses inference rules to derive related elements.

4.2.1 Relational Database Model

The relational model uses tables to organize the data elements. Each table corresponds to an application entity, and each row represents an instance of that entity. For example, the cat entity in the application corresponds to the Cat table in the database. Each table row represents a different cat. Relationships link rows from two tables by embedding row identifiers from one table as attribute values in another table. For example, the identifier of a cat row (the cat name) appears in a student row, thereby establishing the student as the owner of the cat.

Despite complications that arise from relationships involving many rows from many tables, this simple mechanism supports relationships without resorting to auxiliary structures, such as linked lists or indexes. Structured Query Language (SQL) serves as the uniform interface for users, providing a collection of standard expressions for storing and retrieving data.

Relational DBMS products also derived significant benefits from years of database research. The relational model has a rigorous mathematical base. The concept of a relation itself is a mathematical one. Each attribute has an associated domain, and the relation's body at any time is, except for the attribute order, a subset of the Cartesian product of these domains. The mathematical definition of a relation over a finite collection of domains is essentially the same: a subset of the Cartesian product. The only difference is that the relational definition removes the attribute order that is inherent in the mathematical Cartesian product. The model's name, therefore, comes from its mathematical counterpart.

The definitions of the relational database components also proceed from mathematical concepts:

- A relational database is a set of relations, each comprising a schema and a body.
- A relational body is a set of tuples over the corresponding relational schema.
- A tuple over a relational schema is a set of associations over the corresponding attributes.
- A relational schema is a set of attributes.
- An association over an attribute is a name-value pair, where the name comes from the attribute and the value comes from the corresponding domain.
- An attribute is a name-domain pair.
- A domain is a set of values.

The relational model was designed to remove the host-language access requirement and to suppress the subsidiary structures for maintaining relationships. From the user's viewpoint, matching values in common attributes implicitly lace together related tuples in disjoint tables. The DBMS can use indices, linked lists, and other structures to enhance performance, but it hides these technical details from the user.

SQL provides a systematic, nonprocedural interface, which removes the need for the user to understand a host programming language. Although SQL itself is a programming language, it is simple compared to the procedural hosts of the hierarchical and network models. Because it is patterned after structured English, SQL is accessible to a wide range of nontechnical users. Those who have written query solutions for the hierarchical and network models will appreciate the relational model.

Other strengths of a relational DBMS also arose from relational research, which culminated in Codd's 12 rules including the following important criteria:

1. Only table structures are visible to the user.
2. An active catalog stores metadata, which makes the database self-describing.
3. The user interface employs a set-oriented language.
4. A conceptual schema buffers applications from changes to the underlying physical storage.
5. A view mechanism buffers applications from changes in the conceptual schema.

In summary, the relational model's advantages over its predecessors are its simple tabular schema, its uncomplicated relationship representation scheme, its comparatively simple access language, SQL, and its strong mathematical foundation for the underlying concepts.

The relational model has generated its own deficiencies by enabling the exploration of more difficult problem domains, such as databases with pictures and soundtracks. Some difficulties touch on philosophical data modeling issues, such as dispersing an application entity across several tables. Others are simple inconveniences, which seldom provoke practical problems. For example, SQL is not computationally complete, but this deficiency is barely noticed outside of academic textbooks. The postrelational models do, however, address these issues.

4.2.2 Hierarchical Database Model

The hierarchical model assumes that a tree structure, such as the company organizational chart of Figure 4.1, is the most frequently occurring relationship. The president is at the top, over a reporting structure that branches into vice presidents, departments, and employees. Several vice presidents report to the president, and several departments report to each vice president. At the lowest level, each department contains many employees.

A key feature of this organization is that you can translate it into a linear list, as illustrated below.

President (name = jones, phone = 111-222-3333, etc.)
Vice President (name = able, ...)
Department (name = Electrical, ...)
Employee (name = doyle, ...)
Employee (name = erikson, ...)
Employee (name = ferris, ...)
Department (name = Mechanical, ...)
Employee (name = gilbert, ...)
Employee (name = hansen, ...)
Vice President (name = baker, ...)
Department (name = Finance, ...)
Employee (name = jarbo, ...)
Employee (name = karlstrom, ...)
Department (name = Marketing, ...)
Department (name = Accounting, ...)
Employee (name = marchand, ...)

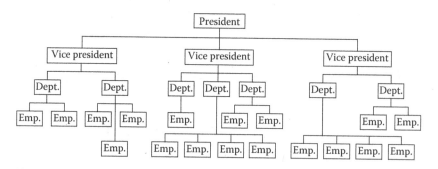

Figure 4.1   A hierarchical organization.

The hierarchical model organizes data elements as tabular rows, one for each instance of an application entity. In this example, a separate row represents the president, each vice president, each department, and each employee. The row position implies a relationship to other rows. That is, a given employee belongs to the department that is closest above him/her in the list; a given department reports to the vice president immediately above it in the list.

The hierarchical model represents relationships with the notion of logical adjacency, or more accurately, with logical proximity, in the linearized tree. You can isolate the set of employees working for departments under vice president X by first locating vice president X and then including every employee in the list after X and before the next occurrence of a vice president (or the end of the list). Because the linearized tree is an abstraction, the term logical proximity is more appropriate. An actual implementation may scatter the data items across various structures and materialize the linearized tree as needed with hashing.

The hierarchical model has overly complicated structures for maintaining relationships. Although logical adjacency is a straightforward organizational principle, it is not sufficient for multiple parentage situations. In these cases, the hierarchical model introduces a second scheme for maintaining relationships—virtual chains. This solution forces an asymmetry into the model: some relationships use logical adjacency, and some use virtual chains. You must remain constantly aware of the distinction when writing navigational queries. Moreover, the hierarchical model involves database designers in yet more programming details because they must direct the DBMS in constructing the type hierarchies. For instance,

- Should the records contain one-way or two-way links?
- Should dependent records contain parent pointers?
- Should the root records enjoy a fast access path, such as a hash table?

These questions are far from the application domain where the designers should be working.

The hierarchical model actually employs the network set concept, disguised as virtual chains, but does not elevate it to full status with appropriate commands for using it. Instead, it mixes database commands with programming language control methods, such as threaded trees. Because the hierarchical model is so tightly bound with a host control language, you must be a capable programmer to use it. Under these conditions, writing database manipulation programs is a difficult and specialized task. The syntax of commercial hierarchical products makes the problem worse because it is typically dense and cryptic, with many references to physical storage details.

The hierarchical and network models share many features.

1. Both represent data as records, and both include navigation commands for moving among related records. Both also express queries and update activities in a host program that makes library procedure calls to transfer information back and forth to the database. These common features lead to common weaknesses.

2. Both the models offset the cumbersome representation of relationships by the relative speed and efficiency. To maintain network sets or virtual relationships, they use pointer chains, which provide direct disk addresses of related records. The application designer can also specify rapid retrieval structures for the logical adjacency implementation, such as pointer arrays, indices, or hash tables. These devices circumvent the sequential search implied by the physical parent–child relationship in the linearized hierarchy. For relationships that are built into the applications, these methods locate the disk addresses of related records with less overhead than in the relational or postrelational models. The lower-level linkage mechanisms increase the efficiency of both these models, they do not make up for the less flexible relationship representation methods. Thus, for ad hoc relationships that appear after the database is in use, the prewired disk address links provide no assistance, and the performance degenerates to sequential searches.

3. Both of the model's access languages are more powerful than SQL. In particular, you can express recursive
queries with unbounded depths. Of course, the price of
this flexibility is long and potentially expensive programming. Moreover, the ability to probe recursive relationships is usually wasted in the hierarchical case because
a hierarchical DBMS typically does not allow recursive
relationships.

4.2.3 Network Database Model

The network model replaces the hierarchical tree with a graph, allowing more general connections among the nodes. Suppose in the previous example that an employee works for two departments. Then
the strict hierarchical arrangement breaks down, and the tree of
Figure 4.1 becomes a more general graph or network. Logical proximity fails, because you cannot place a data item simultaneously in two
locations in the list. Although the hierarchical model contains more
complicated methods to handle these situations, the syntax becomes
difficult to follow. The network database model evolved specifically to
handle nonhierarchical relationships.

The network model corrects the hierarchical model's most trouble-
some oversight—the awkward representation of multiple parentage.
It also raises relationships to the status of named database elements, network sets, and it introduces commands for manipulating them. These
extensions enable more realistic modeling of real-world situations. They
also conform directly with the features of entity-relationship diagrams,
which are currently the most popular database design methods. For a
user interface, however, the network model still uses database calls from
a host language control program. This approach is certainly very flexible because, in theory, you can program any user interface. However,
these programs are expensive and involve a lot of duplicated effort.
Furthermore, they discourage nontechnical users who are not proficient
in the host language. The network model also retains a relationship
maintenance mechanism (i.e., network sets) that exposes the underlying data structures (i.e., linked chains). Because it requires familiarity
with computer science constructs, this feature further limits the number of potential users.

4.2.4 Object-Oriented Database Models

The object-oriented model represents an application entity as a class. A class captures both the attributes and the behavior of the entity. For example, a Cat class possesses not only cat attributes, such as color, weight, and napTime, but also procedures that imitate actions expected of a cat, such as destroyFurniture ("sofa"). Instances of the class, called objects, correspond to individual cats. Within an object, the class attributes take specific values, which distinguish, for example, one cat from another. However, the behavior patterns are shared by all cat objects. The object-oriented model does not restrict attribute values to the small set of native data types usually associated with databases and programming languages, such as integer, float, real, decimal, and string. Instead, the values can be other objects. One of the attributes of a cat can be owner, and the value of that attribute can be a student object, corresponding to the student that owns the cat in the application.

In the object-oriented model, the application entities become database classes, and entity instances become objects under the appropriate class. A class corresponds roughly to a table shell in the relational model, and an object corresponds to a row in the table. A class is actually a more expressive modeling feature than a table because it captures the behavior of its objects in addition to their static attributes. Moreover, an object's attribute values are not limited to the simple strings and numbers of the earlier models: they can be other objects. The DBMS can, therefore, represent an object as a compact structure that contains its related objects; logical inclusion is simpler because it frequently corresponds more naturally with the real-world relationship. By contrast, the relational model visibly maintains related tuples in separate tables. Relationship representation through logical inclusion is at least as straightforward as through common attribute links. Because an application object contains related objects within itself, at some level of recursion, you can construct query solutions by probing the candidate object's attributes. This approach is procedural, so you might suspect it is inferior to the nonprocedural SQL. But the required procedures are, in fact, simple in comparison with the host language programming of the hierarchical and network models.

Furthermore, nonprocedural extensions, such as OQL, salvage much of SQL's convenience while still exploiting the model's object-oriented features.

All the strengths of object-oriented modeling are available in an object-oriented database: inheritance, encapsulation, polymorphism, and message-passing among objects. You can insert application classes at appropriate points in an existing class hierarchy. An object instantiated through an application class then contains not only the attributes and methods defined in that class, but also the attributes and methods of its superclasses. So you can define a new class incrementally by specifying only how it extends its immediate parent.

The object-oriented model possesses the following advantages over its relational predecessor: a class structure, which encapsulates behavior as well as the traditional static attributes; a simple relationship mechanism, logical inclusion, which often corresponds with its real-world equivalent; and application-modeling features adopted from object-oriented software development, such as inheritance and polymorphism. One regression appears to be the reappearance of a host programming language for user access to the database. The object-oriented language syntax is, however, less difficult than the host languages of the earlier models. In any case, a nonprocedural query language, Object Query Language (OQL), is available. OQL retains the flavor of SQL but provides access to the database's object-oriented features.

4.2.5 Comparison of Models

4.2.5.1 Similarities

1. The most obvious similarity is that all five models possess features for storing both application entity descriptions and instances of these entities. Regardless of the database model, an application entity description is an attribute collection; an entity instance is a collection of values under these attributes.

2. To maintain application entities and their instances, all five database models also use some form of table format. Each application entity becomes a separate table. The instances of a given entity become rows in its table. All five database models use some generalization of the table format in this fashion.

The relational model, of course, explicitly specifies tables as the storage mechanism.

a. In a relational schema, you describe a table shell for each application entity. In subsequent processing, you manipulate the table rows as instances of the corresponding application entity.

b. In a hierarchical schema, you specify a segment for each application entity. Except for the notation, however, a segment description is the same as a network record type description. Both contain a list of named fields and imply a file of records that are compatible with the fields.

c. In a network schema, you specify a record type for each application entity. A file of records then represents the instances. A file is a generalized table, where the repeating elements are records rather than rows. Each record, however, corresponds exactly to a row because it is a sequence of field values, just as a row is a sequence of attribute values.

If you broaden the definition of a table to include a file of records, you can conclude that the relational, network, and hierarchical database models all use tables to store the application entities and their instances.

The object-oriented database models can also use tables. However, this model's philosophies de-emphasize storage structure and leave the choice to a given implementation. In the object-oriented model, an application entity becomes a class; the instances become objects created from the corresponding class. A class encapsulates an attribute collection, and each object from the class provides specific values for the attributes. Although the model provides no further storage details, you can still envision the objects as rows in a table. Each row provides the values for the class attributes, which appear across the top of the table. In this representation, the object identifier (OID) is just another attribute.

3. In addition to using tables to store the application entities and their instances, all five database models also provide some arrangement for navigating through relationships to extract

query solutions. The representative structures have evolved from primitive linking schemes that expose the implementation structures to more abstract relationship concepts that suppress implementation detail. In all cases, however, query solutions still exploit the available relationship mechanism to assemble related data elements.

You always solve an existential query by searching for database paths between a candidate and an anchor.

a. Existential queries:

You always solve an existential query by searching for database paths between a candidate and an anchor. Only the details for expressing the path vary from one model to the next.

In the relational model, the path proceeds across one-to-many relationships by linking tuples where the foreign-key value in the dependent entity matches the primary-key value in the dominant entity. In the network model, you construct the path by traversing the record chains of the network sets. This navigation again proceeds across one-to-many relationships because each chain corresponds to a relationship instance, which links a dominant record with its dependent partners. The path can enter on a dominant record and depart from a dependent record, or it can enter on a dependent record and depart from the dominant one. In a hierarchical database, you encounter both physical and virtual one-to-many relationships as you construct the existential path. The process for a virtual relationship is the same as in the network case: you move along linked chains from the dominant to a dependent record or vice versa. For a physical relationship, you move within a linearized hierarchy of records. You move backward to the first record of the proper type to link a dependent record with its dominant partner. You scan forward to obtain the dependents associated with a given dominant record.

In an object-oriented database, an existential path burrows into the candidate's attributes. Because attribute values can be complex objects, this process continually discovers related objects, and it can continue the probe by investigating their attributes. Although the model provides no further implementation detail, you can imagine an existential path passing through table rows, just as in the relational case. Where a relational path jumps from a foreign-key value to a matching primary-key value in a row of a remote table, an object-oriented path jumps from an attribute OID to a matching object in a remote table. This viewpoint, of course, assumes that objects are arrayed in tabular rows as discussed above.

b. Universal queries:

Solving universal queries is also similar for all five models. You construct two sets: the anchors and the elements reachable from a candidate. If the second set includes the first, the candidate contributes to the answer. Only the details of the set constructions vary across the models. Two approaches are available in the relational model: the set-containment approach and the doubly negated approach. In the former, you explicitly construct the two sets with subqueries and then test for containment. In the doubly negated solution, the set containment is tested one element at a time, without explicitly building the sets. Set A is contained in set B if and only if $(\forall x)(x \in A \Rightarrow x \in B)$. Equivalently, set A is contained in set B if and only if $-(\exists x)(x \in A \wedge -(x \in B))$. The two negations produce two not-exists subqueries in the Structured Query Language (SQL) expression. In both the hierarchical, network, and object-oriented models, you must accumulate the two sets in a host language program, which makes appropriate calls to the database. You also test the set containment with the host language features.

c. Aggregate queries:

Aggregate queries involve a summarizing computation over a partitioned table. In the hierarchical, network, and object-oriented models, you explicitly program the calculations in a host language program, which calls the database as needed. The process is implicit in the relational and deductive models, although the DBMS must set up the same partitioning and summarizing activities that you program in the other models.

4.2.5.2 Dissimilarities Within a database, an application object or relationship appears as a data element or grouping of data elements. The relational model is value based; it assumes that a real-world entity has no identity independent of its attribute values. The content of the database record, rather than its existence, determines the identity of the object represented. If a cat changes its attributes sufficiently to represent a mouse, then it is a mouse.

The object-oriented network and hierarchical models assume that the object survives changes of all its attributes; these systems are record based. A record of the real-world entity appears in the database, and even though the record's contents may change completely, the record itself represents the application item. As long as the record remains in the database, the object's identity has not changed (Table 4.1).

Table 4.1 Characteristics of the Four Database Models

MODEL	DATA ELEMENT ORGANIZATION	RELATIONSHIP ORGANIZATION	IDENTITY	ACCESS LANGUAGE
Relational	Tables	Identifiers for rows of one table are embedded as attribute values in another table	Value based	Nonprocedural
Object-oriented	Obejects— logically encapsulating both attributes and behavior	Logical containment, related objects are found within a given object by recursively examining attributes of an object that are themselves objects	Record based	Procedural
Deductive	Base facts that can be arranged in tables	Inference rules that permit related facts to be generated on demand	Value based	Nonprocedural
Hierarchial	Files, records	Logical proximity in a linearized tree	Record based	Procedural
Network	Files, records	Intersecting chains	Record based	Procedural

4.3 Database Components

The database provides three layers of abstraction, each buffered to a certain extent from changes in the layers below:

1. The physical layer deals with storage structures. This layer contains low-level data structures (e.g., files, control blocks, search accelerators), and it accommodates the hardware capabilities. It also provides support services for the conceptual layer.
2. The conceptual layer projects the illusion of tables and objects, from which the user fashions the application environment. The DBMS can protect the conceptual layer from certain changes to the physical layer, a feature known as physical data independence.
3. The top layer represents tailored views of the conceptual layer that are suitable for different users. The DBMS can protect the top layer from limited changes to the conceptual schema, a feature known as logical data independence.

A DBMS contains a module for processing the database schema, which is a script describing the application environment in terms of the structures provided by the model, that is, in terms of tables, objects, inference rules, hierarchical trees, or network chains. The DBMS stores this description as a data dictionary, which it uses to resolve references to application entities that appear in service requests. Another component provides a clean interface to users, hiding the computer structures. The user never faces indices, hash tables, file buffers, and the like. Rather, he/she deals with the tables, objects, axioms, and rules that model the application environment.

4.3.1 Conceptual Level

The highest level of Figure 4.2 presents varying external tailored views of the application to different users. For example, one program may consider cat attributes to be simply name and weight, while another program may expect a more complete definition, including eye color, fur color, and associated student owners. Differing external views can use the same conceptual description to satisfy these differing expectations. Moreover, if a program expects an entity to contain certain attributes, it should be unaffected if the conceptual schema changes to add

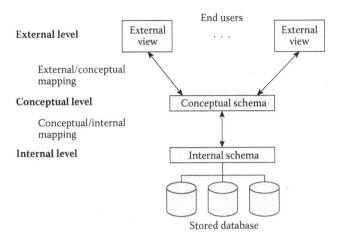

Figure 4.2 The three-schema architecture.

more attributes to the corresponding database object. Of course, certain DBMS parameters may require adjustment to materialize the old external view from a modified conceptual schema. However, the program that uses that old view remains insulated from the change.

4.3.2 Logical Level

Isolating these storage details in the lowest level of the DBMS provides a comfortable buffer for the next higher layer of abstraction, the conceptual level. The application objects exist at this level. If the underlying hardware or operating system changes, the consequences are confined to the interface between the physical layer and the conceptual layer immediately above it. If the database designer is controlling the physical schema, he/she may need to modify and recompile it. In any case, he/she must retune the DBMS to function efficiently in the new environment. In the worst case, this may involve purchasing a new version of the DBMS. For example, if the platform changes from VAX VMS to UNIX (two operating systems), a new version of the DBMS would probably be necessary. The important point is that all applications constructed over the objects in the conceptual layer remain valid. A potentially large investment in application programs that use the database is not affected. The term physical data independence describes this decoupling of the application programs from the underlying hardware and data structures. The three-level diagram of Figure 4.2 illustrates the point.

The middle layer of Figure 4.2 describes the complete application environment in terms of the abstractions supported by the DBMS, such as tables, objects, or inference rules. Here reside the entities of interest in the application, together with their relationships, constraints, and security measures. Just as this layer can remain stable in the face of changes in the physical support layer below it, modifications to this conceptual picture can often be hidden from the next higher level.

4.3.3 Physical Level

At the lowest level, farthest removed from the application entities (e.g., cats, students), certain physical components organize and store the raw data. In addition to the hardware, these components include control structures that track which data elements reside on which disks and in which format. Other structures appear here to also accelerate performance, such as buffers for holding frequently used data and information for conducting rapid searches. The physical layer typically has parameters that can be tuned for optimal performance under the access patterns of a particular application. Therefore, the database designer may want to specify these parameters. However, the later models (i.e., relational, object-oriented, deductive) typically leave the tuning task to the DBMS. If the database designer does have access to these structures, he/she specifies appropriate values in a physical schema. The physical schema is a second machine-readable script, which addresses such issues as what data elements to store in close physical proximity (on the same disk track or cylinder, for example), how to distribute the data across multiple files and storage devices, and which files to index.

4.4 Summary

This chapter presented an overview of the traditional database environments, namely relational, hierarchical, network, and object-oriented databases. Before we embark on a description of business performance and performance intelligence, the remaining chapters of Section II presents an overview of other areas that were significant milestones on the road to performance intelligence, namely data warehousing, data mining, analytics, and business intelligence.

5

DATA WAREHOUSING
SYSTEMS

Decision support systems are interactive, computer-based information systems that provide data and analysis tools in order to assist managers at various levels of an organization in the process of decision-making. Data warehouses have been developed and deployed as an integral part of decision support systems. Data warehouses are increasingly being used by many organizations in many sectors to improve their operations and to better achieve their objectives. For example, a data warehouse application can be used in an organization to analyze customers' behavior; by understanding its customers, the organization is then able to better address their specific needs and expectations.

Data warehouses are databases of a specific kind that periodically collect information about the activities being performed by an organization. This information is then accumulated over a period of time for the purpose of analyzing how it evolves and, thus, for discovering strategic information such as trends, correlations, and the like. A data warehouse is a database that allows the storage of high volumes of historical data required for analytical purposes. These data are extracted from operational databases, transformed into a coherent whole, and loaded into a data warehouse during an extraction-transformation-loading (ETL) process. Data in data warehouses can be dynamically manipulated using online analytical processing (OLAP) systems.

5.1 Relevant Database Concepts

Databases constitute the core component of today's information systems. A database is a shared collection of logically related data, and a description of that data, designed to meet the information needs and support the activities of an organization. A database is deployed on a database management system (DBMS), which is a software system that allows users to define, create, manipulate, and administer a database.

Designing a database system is a complex undertaking that is typically divided into four phases:

1. Requirements specification, which collects information about the users' needs with respect to the database system. A large number of approaches for requirements specification have been developed by both academia and practitioners. In general, these techniques help to elicit necessary and desirable system properties from prospective users and/or project managers, to homogenize requirements, and to assign priorities to them, that is, to separate necessary from "nice to have" system properties. During this phase, active participation of users will increase customer satisfaction with the delivered system and avoid errors, which can be very expensive to correct if the subsequent phases have already been developed.

2. Conceptual design, which aims at building a user-oriented representation of the database that does not contain any implementation considerations. This is done by using a conceptual model in order to identify the relevant entities, relationships, and attributes of the application domain. The entity-relationship model is one of the most often used conceptual models for designing database applications. Alternatively, object-oriented modeling techniques can also be applied, based on UML notation. Conceptual design can be performed using two different approaches, according to the complexity of the system and the developers' experience:

   a. Logical design, which aims at translating the conceptual representation of the database obtained in the previous phase into a particular implementation model (or logical model) common to several DBMS. Currently, the most common logical models are the relational model and the object relational model. Other logical models include the object-oriented model and the semi-structured (or XML-based) model. To ensure an adequate logical representation, suitable mapping rules must be specified. These ensure that the constructs included in the conceptual model can be transformed to the appropriate structures of the logical model.

b. Physical design, which aims at customizing the logical representation of the database obtained in the previous phase to an implementation in a particular DBMS platform. Common DBMS include SQL Server, Oracle, DB2, and MySQL, among others.

5.1.1 Physical Database Design

The objective of physical database design is to specify how database records are stored, accessed, and related in order to ensure the adequate performance of a database application. Physical database design thus requires one to know the specificities of the given application, in particular the properties of the data and the usage patterns of the database. The latter involves analyzing the transactions or queries that are run frequently and will have a significant impact on performance, the transactions that are critical to the operations of the organization, and the periods of time during which there will be a high demand on the database (called the peak load). This information is used to identify the parts of the database that may cause performance problems.

There are a number of factors that can be used to measure the performance of database applications. Transaction throughput is the number of transactions that can be processed in a given time interval. In some systems, such as electronic payment systems, a high transaction throughput is critical. Response time is the elapsed time for the completion of a single transaction. Minimizing response time is essential from the user's point of view.

Finally, disk storage is the amount of disk space required to store the database files. However, a compromise usually has to be made among these factors. From a general perspective, this compromise implies the following factors:

1. *Space-time trade-off*: It is often possible to reduce the time taken to perform an operation by using more space and vice versa. For example, using a compression algorithm allows one to reduce the space occupied by a large file but implies extra time for the decompression process.

2. *Query-update trade-off:* Access to data can be made more efficient by imposing some structure upon it. However, the more elaborate the structure, the more time is taken to build it and to maintain it when its contents change. For example, sorting the records of a file according to a key field allows them to be located more easily but there is a greater overhead upon insertions.

Further, once an initial physical design has been implemented, it is necessary to monitor the system and to tune it as a result of the observed performance and any changes in requirements. Many DBMS provide utilities to monitor and tune the operations of the system. As the functionality provided by current DBMS varies widely, physical design requires one to know the various techniques for storing and finding data that are implemented in the particular DBMS that will be used.

5.2 Data Warehouse

Organizations in all sectors are being required to improve their decision-making processes in order to maintain their competitive advantage. Traditional database systems like the ones studied in Chapter 4 do not satisfy the requirements of data analysis. They are designed and tuned to support the daily operations of an organization, and their primary concern is to ensure fast, concurrent access to data. This requires transaction processing and concurrency control capabilities, as well as recovery techniques that guarantee data consistency. These systems are known as operational databases or online transaction processing (OLTP) systems. The OLTP paradigm is focused on transactions.

In a typical database example, a simple transaction could involve entering a new order, reserving the products ordered, and, if the reorder point has been reached, issuing a purchase order for the required products. Eventually, a user may want to know the status of a given order. If a database is indexed following one of the techniques described in the previous chapter, a typical OLTP query like the above would require accessing only a few records of the database (and normally will return a few tuples). Since OLTP systems must support heavy transaction loads, their design should prevent update anomalies, and thus, OLTP databases are highly normalized. However, they perform poorly when executing complex queries that need to join many relational tables together or to aggregate large volumes of data. Besides, typical operational databases contain detailed data and do not include historical data.

The above need calls for a new paradigm specifically oriented to analyze the data in organizational databases to support decision-making. This paradigm is called online analytical processing (OLAP). This paradigm is focused on queries, in particular, analytical queries. OLAP-oriented databases should support a heavy query load. Typical OLAP queries over the Northwind database would ask, for example, for the total sales amount by product and by customer or for the most ordered products by customer. These kinds of queries involve aggregation, and thus, processing them will require, most of the time, traversing all the records in a database table. Indexing techniques aimed at OLTP are not efficient in this case: new indexing and query optimization techniques are required for OLAP. It is easy to see that normalization is not good for these queries, since it partitions the database into many tables. Reconstructing the data would require a high number of joins (Table 5.1).

Therefore, the need for a different database model to support OLAP was clear and led to the notion of data warehouses, which are (usually) large repositories that consolidate data from different sources (internal and external to the organization), are updated off-line (although this is not always the case in modern data warehouse systems), and follow the multidimensional data model. Being dedicated analysis databases,

Table 5.1 Comparison between OLTP and OLAP Systems

CHARACTERISTIC	OLTP	OLAP
Volatility	Dynamic data	Static data
Timelines	Current data only	Current and historical data
Time dimension	Implicit and current	Explicit and variant
Granularity	Detailed data	Aggregated and consolidated data
Updating	Continuous and irregular	Periodic and regular
Activities	Repetitive	Unpredictable
Flexibility	Low	High
Performance	High, few seconds per query	May be low for complex queries
Users	Employees	Knowledge workers
Functions	Operational	Analytical
Purpose of use	Transactions	Complex queries and decision support
Priority	High performance	High flexibility
Metrics	Transaction rate	Effective response
Size	Megabytes to gigabytes	Gigabytes to terabytes

data warehouses can be designed and optimized to efficiently support OLAP queries. In addition, data warehouses are also used to support other kinds of analysis tasks, like reporting, data mining, and statistical analysis.

A data warehouse is usually defined as a collection of subject-oriented, integrated, nonvolatile, and time-varying data to support management decisions. Thus, the salient features of a data warehouse are that it is:

- Subject-oriented, which means that a data warehouse targets one or several subjects of analysis according to the analytical requirements of managers at various levels of the decision-making process. For example, a data warehouse in a retail company may contain data for the analysis of the purchase, inventory, and sales of products.
- Integrated, which expresses the fact that the contents of a data warehouse result from the integration of data from various operational and external systems.
- Nonvolatile, which indicates that a data warehouse accumulates data from operational systems for a long period of time. Thus, data modification and removal are not allowed in data warehouses: the only operation allowed is the purging of obsolete data that are no longer needed.
- Time-varying, which underlines that a data warehouse keeps track of how its data have evolved over time; for instance, it may allow one to know the evolution of sales or inventory over the last several months or years (Table 5.2).

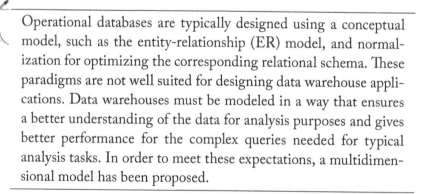

Operational databases are typically designed using a conceptual model, such as the entity-relationship (ER) model, and normalization for optimizing the corresponding relational schema. These paradigms are not well suited for designing data warehouse applications. Data warehouses must be modeled in a way that ensures a better understanding of the data for analysis purposes and gives better performance for the complex queries needed for typical analysis tasks. In order to meet these expectations, a multidimensional model has been proposed.

Table 5.2 Comparison between Operational Databases and Data Warehouses

DESCRIPTION	OPERATIONAL DATABASES	DATA WAREHOUSES
User type	Operators, office employees	Managers, high-ranking executives
Usage	Predictable, repetitive	Ad hoc, nonstructured
Data content	Current, detailed data	Historical, summarized data
Data organization	According to operational needs	According to the analysis problem
Data structures	Optimized for small transactions	Optimized for complex queries
Access frequency	High	From medium to low
Access type	Read, update, delete, insert	Read, append only
Number of records per access	Few	Many
Response time	Short	Can be long
Concurrency level	High	Low
Lock utilization	Necessary	Not necessary
Update frequency	High	None
Data redundancy	Low (normalized tables)	High (unnormalized tables)
Data modeling	ER model	Multidimensional model
Modeling and implementation	Entire system	Incremental

5.2.1 Multidimensional Model

Data warehouse and OLAP systems rely on a multidimensional model that includes measures, dimensions, and hierarchies:

- Measures are usually numeric values that are used for quantitative evaluation of aspects of an organization.
- Dimensions provide various analysis perspectives.
- Hierarchies allow measures to be analyzed at various levels of detail.

The multidimensional model views data as consisting of facts linked to several dimensions:

1. Facts represent a focus of analysis (e.g., analysis of sales in stores) and typically include attributes called measures.
2. Measures are usually numeric values that allow quantitative evaluation of various aspects of an organization to be performed. For example, measures such as the amount or quantity of sales might help to analyze sales activities in various stores.
3. Dimensions are used to see the measures from different perspectives. For example, a time dimension can be used for analyzing changes in sales over various periods of time, whereas

a location dimension can be used to analyze sales according to the geographic distribution of stores. Users may combine several different analysis perspectives (i.e., dimensions) according to their needs. For example, a user may require information about sales of computer accessories (the product dimension) in June 2016 (the time dimension) in all store locations (the store dimension). Dimensions typically include attributes that form hierarchies, which allow decision-making users to explore measures at various levels of detail. Examples of hierarchies are month–quarter–year in the time dimension and city–state–country in the location dimension.

4. Hierarchies allow measures to be analyzed at various levels of detail; when a hierarchy is traversed, aggregation of measures takes place. For example, moving in a hierarchy from a month level to a year level will yield aggregated values of sales for the various years.

5.2.1.1 Data Cube   A data cube is defined by dimensions and facts. Dimensions are various perspectives that are used to analyze the data. For example, the data cube in Figure 5.1 is used to analyze sales figures and has three dimensions: Store, Time, and Product. Instances of a dimension are called members. For example, Chennai, Kolkata, Delhi, and Mumbai are members of the Store dimension. Dimensions have associated attributes describing the dimension. For example, the Product dimension could contain attributes such as Product Number, Product Name, Description, and Size, which are not shown in the figure. On the other hand, the cells of a data cube, or facts, have associated with them numeric values, called measures. These measures allow quantitative evaluation of various aspects of the analysis problem at hand to be performed. For example, the numbers shown in the data cube in Figure 5.1 represent a measure amount, indicating the total sales amount specified in, for instance, thousands of euros. A data cube typically contains several measures. For example, another measure, not shown in the cube in Figure 5.1, could be quantity, representing the number of units sold.

A data cube may be sparse or dense depending on whether it has measures associated with each combination of dimension values.

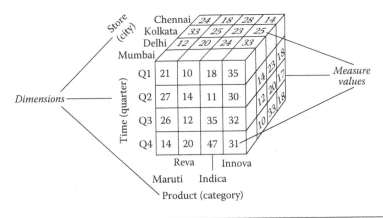

Figure 5.1   Cube for sales data having the dimensions Store, Time, and Product and a measure amount.

In the case of Figure 5.1, this depends on whether all products are sold in all stores throughout the period of time considered. The figure shows two empty cells for the sales in Mumbai of Reva and Indica during the second and third quarters, respectively. In real-world applications, it is common to have sparse cubes. Adequately managing sparsity allows the required storage space to be reduced and improves query performance.

5.2.1.2 Online Analytical Processing (OLAP)   OLAP analyses are based on hierarchies of concepts to consolidate the data and to create logical views along the dimensions of a data warehouse. A concept hierarchy defines a set of maps from a lower level of concepts to a higher level. For example, the {location} dimension may originate a totally ordered hierarchy developing along the {address, municipality, province, country} relationship. The temporal dimension, on the other hand, originates a partially ordered hierarchy, also shown in Figure 5.2.

Specific hierarchy types may be predefined in the software platform used for the creation and management of a data warehouse, as in the case of the dimensions shown in Figure 5.2. For other hierarchies, it is necessary for analysts to explicitly define the relationships among concepts. Hierarchies of concepts are also used to perform several visualization operations dealing with data cubes in a data warehouse.

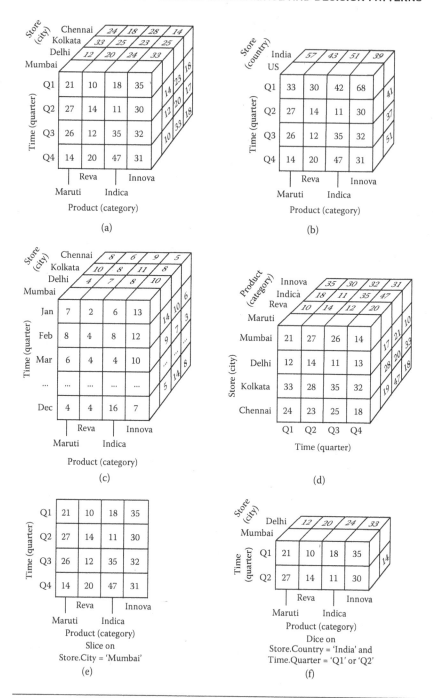

Figure 5.2 OLAP operations. (a) Original cube. (b) Roll up to the country level. (c) Drill down to the month level. (d) Pivot. (e) Slice on Store.City = "Mumbai." (f) Dice on Store.Country = "India" and Time.Quarter = "Q1" or "Q2."

1. *Roll-up*: A roll-up operation, also termed drill-up, consists of an aggregation of data in the cube, which can be obtained alternatively in the following two ways.
   - Proceeding upward to a higher level along a single dimension defined over a concepts hierarchy. For example, for the {location} dimension it is possible to move upward from the {city} level to the {province} level and to consolidate the measures of interest through a group-by conditioned sum over all records whereby the city belongs to the same province.
   - Reducing by one dimension. For example, the removal of the {time} dimension leads to consolidated measures through the sum over all time periods existing in the data cube.
2. *Roll-down*: A roll-down operation, also referred to as drill-down, is the opposite operation to roll-up. It allows navigation through a data cube from aggregated and consolidated information to more detailed information. The effect is to reverse the result achieved through a roll-up operation. A drill-down operation can therefore be carried out in two ways.
   - Shifting down to a lower level along a single dimension hierarchy. For example, in the case of the {location} dimension, it is possible to shift from the {province} level to the {city} level and to disaggregate the measures of interest over all records whereby the city belongs to the same province.
   - Adding one dimension. For example, the introduction of the {time} dimension leads to disaggregation of the measures of interest over all time periods existing in a data cube.
3. *Slice and dice*: Through the slice operation the value of an attribute is selected and fixed along one dimension.
4. *Pivot*: The pivot operation, also referred to as rotation, produces a rotation of the axes, swapping some dimensions to obtain a different view of a data cube.

Although current OLAP systems are based on a multidimensional model, that is, they allow one to represent facts, measures, dimensions, and hierarchies, they are quite restrictive in the types of hierarchies that they can manage. This in an important drawback, since the specification of hierarchies in OLAP systems is important if one is to be able to perform automatic aggregation of measures while traversing hierarchies. OLAP systems allow end users to perform dynamic manipulation and automatic aggregation of the data contained in data warehouses. They facilitate the formulation of complex queries that may involve very large amounts of data. These data are examined and aggregated in order to find patterns or trends of importance to the organization.

OLAP systems have typically been implemented using:

1. Relational OLAP (ROLAP), which stores data in a relational database management system
2. Multidimensional OLAP (MOLAP), which uses a vendor-specific array data structure
3. Hybrid OLAP (HOLAP) systems, which are a combination of ROLAP and MOLAP, for instance using ROLAP for detailed fact data and MOLAP for aggregated data.

5.2.2 Relational Schemas

The multidimensional model is usually represented by relational tables organized in specialized structures called star schemas and snowflake schemas. These relational schemas relate a fact table to several dimension tables. Star schemas use a unique table for each dimension, even in the presence of hierarchies, which yields denormalized dimension tables. On the other hand, snowflake schemas use normalized tables for dimensions and their hierarchies. These are described below.

1. Star Schema

   A star schema has only one central fact table, and a set of dimension tables, one for each dimension. An example is given in Figure 5.3, where the fact table is depicted in gray and the dimension tables are depicted in white. As shown in the figure, referential integrity constraints are specified between the fact table and each of the dimension tables. In a star schema, the dimension tables may contain redundancy, especially in the presence of hierarchies: the tables are not necessarily normalized. This is the case for the dimensions Product and Store in Figure 5.3. Indeed, all products belonging to the same category will have redundant information for the attributes describing the category and

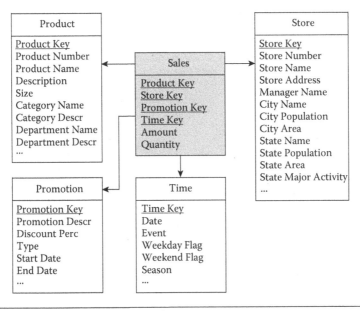

Figure 5.3 Example of a star schema.

the department. The situation is similar for the dimension Store with respect to the attributes describing the city and the state.

2. Snowflake Schema

A snowflake schema avoids the redundancy of star schemas by normalizing the dimension tables. Therefore, a dimension is represented by several tables related by referential integrity constraints. In addition, as in the case of star schemas, referential integrity constraints also relate the fact table and the dimension tables at the finest level of detail. An example of a snowflake schema is given in Figure 5.4, where the dimensions Product and Store are represented by normalized tables. Normalized tables are easy to maintain and allow storage space to be optimized. However, a disadvantage is that performance is affected, since more joins need to be performed when executing queries that require hierarchies to be traversed.

3. Constellation Schema

A constellation schema has multiple fact tables that share dimension tables. The example given in Figure 5.5 has two fact tables Sales and Purchases sharing the Time and Product dimension. Constellation schemas may include both normalized and unnormalized dimension tables.

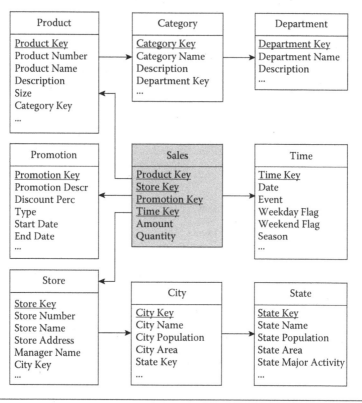

Figure 5.4 Example of a snowflake schema.

5.2.3 Multidimensional Cube

Multidimensional cubes are a natural extension of the popular two-dimensional spreadsheets, which can be interpreted as two-dimensional cubes. A fact table connected with *n* dimension tables may be represented by an *n*-dimensional data cube where each axis corresponds to a dimension. For instance, consider a sales fact table developed along the three dimensions of {time, product, city}. Suppose we select only two dimensions for the analysis, such as {time, product}, having preset the city attribute along the three values {Mumbai, Delhi, Kolkata}. In this way, we obtain the three two-dimensional tables in which the rows correspond to quarters of a year and the columns to products. The cube shown in Figure 5.1 is a three-dimensional illustration of the same sales fact table. Atomic data are represented by 36 cells that can be obtained by crossing all possible values along the three dimensions: time {Q1, Q2, Q3, Q4},

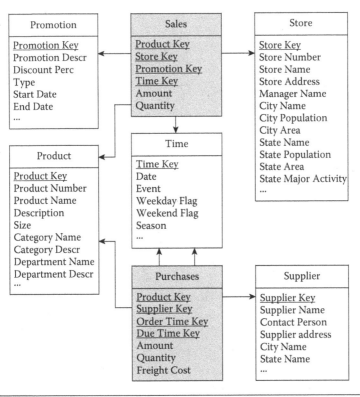

Figure 5.5 Example of a constellation schema.

region {Mumbai, Delhi, Kolkata} and product {Reva, Indica, Innova}. These atomic cells can be supplemented by 44 cells corresponding to the summary values obtained through consolidation along one or more dimensions.

If the sales fact table also contains a fourth dimension represented by the suppliers, the corresponding four-dimensional space cannot be represented graphically; however, four logical views composed of three-dimensional cubes, called cuboids, inside the four-dimensional cube, by fixing the values of one of the dimensions. More generally, starting from a fact table linked to n dimension tables, it is possible to obtain a lattice of cuboids, each of them corresponding to a different level of consolidation along one or more dimensions. This type of aggregation is equivalent in SQL to a query sum derived from a group-by condition. Figure 5.6 illustrates the lattice composed of the cuboids obtained from the data cube defined along the four dimensions {time, product, city, supplier}.

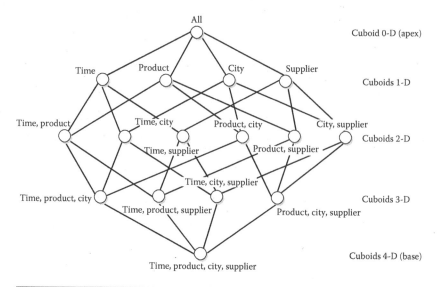

Figure 5.6 Lattice of cuboids derived from a four-dimensional cube.

OLAP analyses developed by knowledge workers may need to access the information associated with several cuboids, based on the specific queries and analyses being carried out. In order to guarantee adequate response time, it might be useful to design a data warehouse where all (or at least a large portion of) values of the measures of interest associated with all possible cuboids are precalculated. This approach is termed full materialization of the information relative to the data cubes.

Observe that where hierarchies of concepts are missing, it is possible to form 2^n distinct cuboids from all possible combinations of n dimensions. The existence of hierarchies along different dimensions makes the number of distinct cuboids even greater. If L_i denotes the number of hierarchical levels associated with the ith dimension, for an n-dimensional data cube it is possible to calculate the full number of cuboids, given by

$$T = \prod_{i=1}^{n} (L_i + 1)$$

For example, if a data cube includes five dimensions, and if each of these dimensions includes three hierarchical levels, the number of cuboids is equal to

$$4^5 = 2^{10} \approx 10^3.$$

It is clear that the full materialization of the cuboids for all the cubes associated with the fact tables of a data warehouse would impose storage requirements that could be hardly sustained over time, considering the rate at which new records or data are generated.

For all of the above reasons, it is necessary to strike a balance between the need for fast access to information, which would suggest the full materialization of the cuboids, and the need to keep memory use within reasonable limits. As a consequence, preventive materialization should be carried out only for those cuboids that are most frequently accessed, while for the others the computation should be carried out on demand only when actual queries requesting the associated information are performed. This latter approach is referred to as partial materialization of the information relative to the data cubes.

5.3 Data Warehouse Architecture

5.3.1 Architecture Tiers

A typical architecture of a data warehouse system consists of several tiers.

5.3.1.1 Back-End Tier The back-end tier is composed of extraction-transformation-loading (ETL) tools, used to feed data in from operational databases and other data sources, which can be internal or external, and a data staging area, which is an intermediate database where all the data integration and transformation processes are run prior to the loading of the data into the data warehouse.

In the back-end tier, the process commonly known as ETL is performed. As the name indicates, it is a three-step process as follows:

- Extraction gathers data from multiple, heterogeneous data sources. These sources may be operational databases but may also be files in various formats; they may be internal to the organization or external to it. In order to solve interoperability problems, data are extracted whenever possible using application program interfaces such as ODBC (Open Database Connection), OLEDB (Open Linking and Embedding for Databases), and JDBC (Java Database Connectivity).

• Transformation modifies the data from the format of the data sources to the warehouse format. This includes several aspects: cleaning, which removes errors and inconsistencies in the data and converts them into a standardized format; integration, which reconciles data from different data sources, both at the schema and at the data level; and aggregation, which summarizes the data obtained from data sources according to the level of detail, or granularity, of the data warehouse.

• Loading feeds the data warehouse with the transformed data. This also includes refreshing the data warehouse, that is, propagating updates from the data sources to the data warehouse at a specified frequency in order to provide up-to-date data for the decision-making process. Depending on organizational policies, the refresh frequency may vary from monthly to several times a day, or even to nearly in real time.

The ETL process usually requires a data staging area, that is, a database in which the data extracted from the sources undergo successive modifications so they are ready for loading into the data warehouse.

5.3.1.2 Data Warehouse Tier   The data warehouse tier is composed of an enterprise data warehouse and/or several data marts, and a metadata repository storing information about the data warehouse and its contents.

The data warehouse tier in Figure 5.7 depicts an enterprise data warehouse and several data marts.

1. The enterprise data warehouse is a centralized data warehouse that encompasses all functional or departmental areas in an organization.
2. The data mart is a specialized data warehouse targeted toward a particular functional area or user group in an organization. A data mart can be seen as a small, local data warehouse. The data in a data mart can be either derived from an enterprise data warehouse or collected directly from data sources.

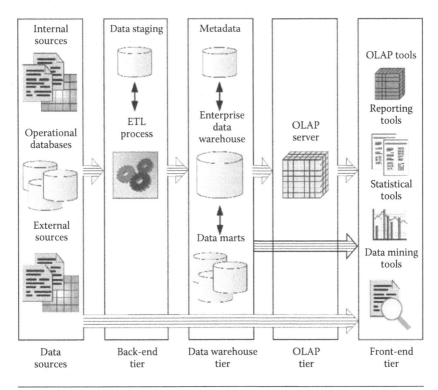

Figure 5.7 Reference data warehouse architecture.

Another component of the data warehouse tier is the metadata repository. Metadata can be defined as "data about data."

1. Business metadata describes the meaning (or semantics) of the data and organizational rules, policies, and constraints related to the data.
2. Technical metadata describes how data is structured and stored in a computer system, and the applications and processes that manipulate the data.

In the data warehouse context, technical metadata can be of various types, describing the data warehouse system, the source systems, and the ETL process. In particular, the metadata repository may contain information such as the following:

• Metadata describing the structure of the data warehouse and the data marts, both at the logical level (which includes the facts, dimensions, hierarchies, derived data definitions, etc.)

and at the physical level (such as indexes, partitions, and replication). In addition, they contain security information (user authorization and access control) and monitoring information (such as usage statistics, error reports, and audit trails).

- Metadata describing the data sources, including their schemas (at the conceptual, logical, and/or physical levels), and descriptive information such as ownership, update frequencies, legal limitations, and access methods.
- Metadata describing the ETL process, including data lineage (i.e., tracing warehouse data back to the source data from which they were derived), data extraction, cleaning, transformation rules and defaults, data refresh and purging rules, algorithms for summarization, etc.

5.3.1.3 OLAP Tier The OLAP tier is an OLAP server that supports multidimensional data and operations.

The OLAP tier in the architecture of Figure 5.7 is composed of an OLAP server that presents business users with multidimensional data from data warehouses or data marts. As already stated, there are several types of OLAP servers depending on the underlying implementation model: ROLAP, MOLAP, and HOLAP.

5.3.1.4 Front-End Tier The front-end tier deals with data analysis and visualization. It contains client tools such as OLAP tools, reporting tools, statistical tools, and data-mining tools.

The front-end tier in Figure 5.7 contains the client tools that allow users to exploit the contents of the data warehouse. Typical client tools include the following:

- OLAP tools that allow interactive exploration and manipulation of the warehouse data in order to identify patterns or trends of importance to the organization. They facilitate the formulation of complex queries that may involve large amounts of data. These queries are called ad hoc queries, since the system has no prior knowledge about them.
- Reporting tools that enable the production, delivery, and management of reports, which can be paper-based reports or

interactive, web-based reports. Reports use predefined queries, that is, queries asking for specific information in a specific format that are performed on a regular basis.

- Statistical tools that are used to analyze and visualize the cube
  data using statistical methods.
- Data-mining tools that allow users to analyze data in order to
  discover valuable knowledge such as patterns and trends; they
  also allow predictions to be made on the basis of current data.

5.4 Summary

This chapter presented the basics of data warehousing. It introduced
the concept of data warehouse and its characteristics, aspects of data
warehouse design including multidimensional models and relational
schemas such as star, snowflake, and constellation schemas. The
later part of the chapter described the generic architecture of a data
warehouse.

6
DATA MINING SYSTEMS

Data mining is widely used by banking firms in soliciting credit card customers, by insurance and telecommunication companies in detecting fraud, by telephone companies and credit card issuers in identifying those potential customers most likely to churn, by manufacturing firms in quality control, and by many other applications. Data mining is being applied to improve food and drug product safety and the detection of terrorists or criminals. Data mining involves statistical and/or artificial intelligence (AI) analysis, usually applied to large-scale datasets. Masses of data generated from cash registers, from scanning, from topic-specific databases throughout companies are explored, analyzed, reduced, and reused. Searches are performed across different models proposed for predicting sales, marketing response, and profit. Although automated AI methods are also used, classic statistical approaches are fundamental to data mining.

Data mining tools need to be versatile, scalable, capable of accurately predicting responses between actions and results, and capable of automatic implementation. Versatile refers to the ability of the tool to apply a wide variety of models. Scalable tools imply that if the tools work on a small dataset, they should also work on larger datasets. Automation is useful, but its application is relative. Some analytic functions are often automated, but human setup prior to implementing procedures is required. In fact, analyst judgment is critical to successful implementation of data mining. Proper selection of data to include in searches is critical: too many variables produce too much output, while too few can overlook key relationships in the data. Data transformation also is often required.

Data mining software products that are being used include Enterprise Miner by SAS, Intelligent Miner by IBM, CLEMENTINE by SPSS, and PolyAnalyst by Megaputer. WEKA (from the University of Waikato in New Zealand) is an open source tool with many useful developing methods.

6.1 Data Mining

Traditional statistical analysis involves an approach that is usually directed, in that a specific set of expected outcomes exists. This approach is referred to as supervised (hypothesis development and testing). But data mining also involves a spirit of knowledge discovery (learning new and useful things). Knowledge discovery is referred to as unsupervised (knowledge discovery). Knowledge discovery by humans can be enhanced by graphical tools and identification of unexpected patterns through a combination of human and computer interaction.

Much of this can be also accomplished through automatic means. A variety of analytic computer models have been used in data mining. The standard models employed in data mining include regression (e.g., normal regression for prediction and logistic regression for classification), neural networks, and so on. This chapter discusses techniques such as association rules for initial data exploration, fuzzy data mining approaches, rough set models, and genetic algorithms. Data mining requires identification of a problem, along with collection of data that can lead to better understanding, and computer models to provide statistical or other means of analysis. This may be supported by visualization tools, that display data, or through fundamental statistical analysis, such as correlation analysis.

Data mining aims to extract knowledge and insight through the analysis of large amounts of data using sophisticated modeling techniques; it converts data into knowledge and actionable information. Data mining models consist of a set of rules, equations, or complex functions that can be used to identify useful data patterns, and understand and predict behaviors.

Data mining is a process that uses a variety of data analysis methods to discover the unknown, unexpected, interesting, and relevant patterns and relationships in data that may be used to make valid and accurate predictions. In general, there are two methods of data analysis: supervised and unsupervised. In both cases, a sample of observed data is required. These data may be termed the training sample. The training sample is used by the data mining activities to learn the patterns in the data.

Data mining models are of two kinds:

1. *Directed or Supervised Models*: In these models, there are input fields or attributes and an output or target field. Input fields are also called predictors because they are used by the model to identify a prediction function for the output or target field. The model generates an *input–output* mapping function, which associates predictors with the output so that, given the values of input fields, it predicts the output values. Predictive models themselves are of two types, namely classification or propensity models and estimation models. Classification models are predictive models with predefined target fields or classes or groups, so that the objective is to predict a specific occurrence or event. The model also assigns a propensity score with each of these events that indicates the likelihood of the occurrence of that event. In contrast, estimation models are used to predict a continuum of target values based on the corresponding input values.

   For instance, a supervised model is used to estimate an unknown dependency from known input–output data.

   a. Input variables might include:
      • Quantities of different articles bought by a particular customer
      • Date of purchase
      • Location
      • Price
   b. Output variables might include an indication of whether the customer responds to a sales campaign or not. Output variables are also known as targets in data mining.

      Sample input variables are passed through a learning system, and the subsequent output from the learning system is compared with the output from the sample.

In other words, we try to predict who will respond to a sales campaign. The difference between the learning system output and the sample output can be thought of as an error signal. Error signals are used to adjust the learning system. This process is done many times with the data from the sample, and the learning system is adjusted until the output meets a minimal error threshold.

2. *Undirected or Unsupervised models*: In these models, there are input fields or attributes, but no output or target field. The goal of such models is to uncover data patterns in the set of input fields. Undirected models are also of two types, namely cluster models and association and sequence models. Cluster models do not have predefined target fields or classes or groups, but the algorithms analyze the input data patterns and identify the natural groupings of cases. In contrast, association or sequence models do not involve or deal with the prediction of a single field. Association models detect associations between discrete events, products, or attributes; sequence models detect associations over time.

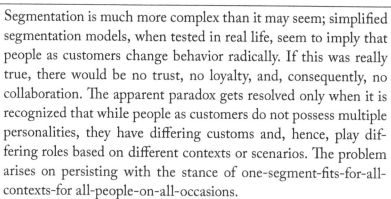

Segmentation is much more complex than it may seem; simplified segmentation models, when tested in real life, seem to imply that people as customers change behavior radically. If this was really true, there would be no trust, no loyalty, and, consequently, no collaboration. The apparent paradox gets resolved only when it is recognized that while people as customers do not possess multiple personalities, they have differing customs and, hence, play differing roles based on different contexts or scenarios. The problem arises on persisting with the stance of one-segment-fits-for-all-contexts-for all-people-on-all-occasions.

Unsupervised data analysis does not involve any fine-tuning. Data mining algorithms search through the data to discover patterns, and there is no target or aim variable. Only input values are presented to the learning system without the need for validation against any output. The goal of unsupervised data analysis is to discover "natural" structures in the input data. In biological systems, perception is a task learnt via an unsupervised technique.

6.1.1 Benefits

Data mining can provide customer insight, which is vital for establishing an effective customer relationship management (CRM) strategy. It can lead to personalized interactions with customers and hence increased satisfaction and profitable customer relationships through data analysis. It can support *individualized* and optimized customer management throughout all the phases of the customer life cycle, from the acquisition and establishment of a strong relationship to the prevention of attrition and the winning back of lost customers.

1. *Segmentation*: This is the process of dividing the customer base into distinct and internally homogeneous groups in order to develop differentiated marketing strategies according to their characteristics. There are many different segmentation types based on the specific criteria or attributes used for segmentation. In behavioral segmentation, customers are grouped by behavioral and usage characteristics. Data mining can uncover groups with distinct profiles and characteristics and lead to rich segmentation schemes with business meaning and value. Clustering algorithms can analyze behavioral data, identify the natural groupings of customers, and suggest a solution founded on observed data patterns.

    Data mining can also be used for the development of segmentation schemes based on the current or expected/estimated value of the customers. These segments are necessary in order to prioritize customer handling and marketing interventions according to the importance of each customer.

2. *Direct Marketing Campaigns*: Marketers use direct marketing campaigns to communicate a message to their customers through mail, the internet, email, telemarketing (phone), and other direct channels in order to prevent churn (attrition) and to drive customer acquisition and purchase of add-on products. More specifically, acquisition campaigns aim at drawing new and potentially valuable customers away from the competition. Cross-/deep-/up-selling campaigns are implemented to sell additional products, more of the same product, or alternative but more profitable products to existing customers. Finally, retention campaigns aim at preventing

valuable customers from terminating their relationship with the organization.

Although potentially effective, this can also lead to a huge waste of resources and to bombarding and annoying customers with unsolicited communications. Data mining and classification (propensity) models in particular can support the development of targeted marketing campaigns. They analyze customer characteristics and recognize the profiles or extended profiles of the target customers.

3. *Market Basket Analysis*: Data mining and association models in particular can be used to identify related products typically purchased together. These models can be used for market basket analysis and for revealing bundles of products or services that can be sold together.

However, to succeed with CRM, organizations need to gain insight into customers, their needs, and wants through data analysis. This is where analytical CRM comes in. Analytical CRM is about analyzing customer information to better address the CRM objectives and deliver the right message to the right customer. It involves the use of data mining models in order to assess the value of the customers, and understand and predict their behavior. It is about analyzing data patterns to extract knowledge for optimizing the customer relationships. For example,

- Data mining can help in customer retention as it enables the timely identification of valuable customers with an increased likelihood of leaving, allowing time for targeted retention campaigns.
- Data mining can support customer development by matching products with customers and better targeting of product promotion campaigns.
- Data mining can also help to reveal distinct customer segments, facilitating the development of customized new products and product offerings, which better address the specific preferences and priorities of the customers.

The results of the analytical CRM procedures should be loaded and integrated into operational CRM frontline systems so that all customer interactions can be more effectively handled on a more informed and personalized base.

6.2 Data Mining Applications

Data mining can be used by businesses in many ways; two of the most profitable application areas have been the use of customer segmentation by marketing organizations to identify those with marginally greater probabilities of responding to different forms of marketing media, and banks using data mining to more accurately predict the likelihood of people to respond to offers of different services offered.

Table 6.1 shows general application areas of data mining.

Many companies are using this data mining to identify their "valuable" customers so that they can provide them with the service needed to retain them by using:

1. Customer profiling, identifying those subsets of customers most profitable to the business
2. Targeting, determining the characteristics of profitable customers who have been captured by competitors
3. Market-basket analysis, determining product purchases by consumer, which can be used for product positioning and for cross-selling

The key is to find actionable information or information that can be utilized in a concrete way to improve profitability. Some of the earliest applications were in retailing, especially in the form of market basket analysis.

Data mining methodologies can be applied to a variety of domains, from marketing and manufacturing process control to the study of

Table 6.1 Data Mining Application Areas

APPLICATION AREA	APPLICATIONS	SPECIFICS
Human resource management	Churn	Identify potential employee turnover
Credit card management	Lift	Identify effective market segments
	Churn	Identify likely customer turnover
Retailing	Affinity positioning, Cross-selling	Position products effectively Find more products for customers
Banking	Customer relationship management	Identify customer value Develop programs to maximize revenue
Insurance	Fraud detection	Identify claims meriting investigation
Telecommunications	Churn	Identify likely customer turnover
Telemarketing	Online information	Aid telemarketers with easy data

risk factors in medical diagnosis, from the evaluation of the effectiveness of new drugs to fraud detection.

1. *Relational marketing*: It is useful for numerous tasks like the identification of customer segments that are most likely to respond to targeted marketing campaigns, such as cross-selling and up-selling; identification of target customer segments for retention campaigns; prediction of the rate of positive responses to marketing campaigns; and interpretation and understanding of the buying behavior of the customers.

2. *Text mining*: Data mining can be applied to different kinds of texts, which represent unstructured data, in order to classify articles, books, documents, emails, and web pages. Examples are web search engines or the automatic classification of press releases for storing purposes. Other text mining applications include the generation of filters for email messages and newsgroups.

3. *Web mining*: It is useful for the analysis of so-called clickstreams—the sequences of pages visited and the choices made by a web surfer. They may prove useful for the analysis of e-commerce sites, in offering flexible and customized pages to surfers, in caching the most popular pages or in evaluating the effectiveness of an e-learning training course.

4. *Image recognition*: The treatment and classification of digital images, both static and dynamic, is useful to recognize written characters, compare and identify human faces, apply correction filters to photographic equipment, and detect suspicious behaviors through surveillance video cameras.

5. *Medical diagnosis*: Learning models are an invaluable tool within the medical field for the early detection of diseases using clinical test results.

6. *Image analysis*: Image analysis for diagnostic purpose is another field of investigation that is currently growing strongly.

7. *Fraud detection*: Fraud detection is relevant for different industries such as telephony, insurance (false claims), and banking (illegal use of credit cards and bank checks; illegal monetary transactions).

8. *Risk evaluation*: The purpose of risk analysis is to estimate the risk connected with future decisions. For example, using the past observations available, a bank may develop a predictive model to establish if it is appropriate to grant a monetary loan or a home loan, based on the characteristics of the applicant.

6.3 Data Mining Analysis

6.3.1 Supervised Analysis

6.3.1.1 Exploratory Analysis This data mining task is primarily conducted by means of exploratory data analysis and therefore it is based on queries and counts that do not require the development of specific learning models. The information so acquired is usually presented to users in the form of histograms and other types of charts.

Before starting to develop a classification model, it is often useful to carry out an exploratory analysis whose purpose is:

- To achieve a characterization by comparing the distribution of the values of the attributes for the records belonging to the same class
- To detect a difference, through a comparison between the distribution of the values of the attributes for the records of a given class and the records of a different class (or between the records of a given class and all remaining records)

The primary purpose of exploratory data analysis is to highlight the relevant features of each attribute contained in a dataset, using graphical methods and calculating summary statistics, and to identify the intensity of the underlying relationships among the attributes. Exploratory data analysis includes three main phases:

1. Univariate analysis, in which the properties of each single attribute of a dataset are investigated
2. Bivariate analysis, in which pairs of attributes are considered to measure the intensity of the relationship existing between them (for supervised learning models, it is of particular

interest to analyze the relationships between the explanatory attributes and the target variable)

3. Multivariate analysis, in which the relationships holding within a subset of attributes are investigated

6.3.1.2 Classification In a classification problem, a set of observations is available, usually represented by the records of a dataset whose target class is known. Observations may correspond, for instance, to mobile phone customers and the binary class may indicate whether a given customer is still active or has churned. Each observation is described by a given number of attributes whose value is known; in the previous example, the attributes may correspond to age, customer seniority and outgoing telephone traffic distinguished by destination. A classification algorithm can therefore use the available observations relative to the past in order to identify a model that can predict the target class of future observations whose attributes values are known.

The target attribute, whose value is to be predicted, is categorical in classification problems and therefore takes on a finite and usually rather small number of values. If the target is a binary variable, in most applications the target is even represented by a binary variable. Classification is intended for discrete targets, when the target variable takes on continuous values it is part of regression analysis. Classification models are supervised learning methods for predicting the value of a categorical target attribute, unlike regression models which deal with numerical attributes. Starting from a set of past observations whose target class is known, classification models are used to generate a set of rules that allow the target class of future examples to be predicted.

Classification analysis has many applications in selection of the target customers for a marketing campaign. Fraud detection, image recognition, early diagnosis of diseases, text cataloguing, and spam email recognition are just a few examples of real problems that can be framed within the classification paradigm.

6.3.1.3 Regression If one wishes to predict the sales of a product based on the promotional campaigns mounted and the sale price, the target variable may take on a very high number of discrete values and can be treated as a continuous variable; this would become a case of regression analysis. Based on the available explanatory attributes, the goal is to predict the value of the target variable for each observation. A classification problem may be effectively turned into a regression problem and vice versa; for instance, a mobile phone company interested in the classification of customers based on their loyalty may come up with a regression problem by predicting the probability of each customer remaining loyal.

The purpose of regression models is to identify a functional relationship between the target variable and a subset of the remaining attributes contained in the dataset. Regression models

- Serve to interpret the dependency of the target variable on the other variables
- Are used to predict the future value of the target attribute, based upon the functional relationship identified and the future value of the explanatory attributes

The development of a regression model allows knowledge workers to acquire a deeper understanding of the phenomenon analyzed and to evaluate the effects determined on the target variable by different combinations of values assigned to the remaining attributes. This is of great interest, particularly for analyzing those attributes that are control levers available to decision makers.

Thus, a regression model may be aimed at interpreting the sales of a product based on investments made in advertising in different media, such as daily newspapers, magazines, TV, and radio. Decision makers may use the model to assess the relative importance of the various communication channels, therefore directing future investments toward those media that appear to be more effective. Moreover, they can also use the model to predict the effects on the sales determined by different marketing policies, so as to design a combination of promotional initiatives that appear to be the most advantageous.

6.3.1.4 Time Series Sometimes the target attribute evolves over time and is therefore associated with adjacent periods on the time axis. In this case, the sequence of values of the target variable is said to represent a time series. For instance, the weekly sales of a given product observed over 2 years represent a time series containing 104 observations. Models for time series analysis investigate data characterized by a temporal dynamics and are aimed at predicting the value of the target variable for one or more future periods.

The aim of models for time series analysis is to identify any regular pattern of observations relative to the past, with the purpose of making predictions for future periods. Time series analysis has many applications in business, financial, socioeconomic, environmental, and industrial domains; predictions may refer to future sales of products and services, and trends in economic and financial indicators, or sequences of measurements relative to ecosystems, for example.

6.3.2 Unsupervised Analysis

6.3.2.1 Association Rules Association rules, also known as affinity groupings, are used to identify interesting and recurring associations between groups of records of a dataset. For example, it is possible to determine which products are purchased together in a single transaction and how frequently. Companies in the retail industry resort to association rules to design the arrangement of products on shelves or in catalogs. Groupings by related elements are also used to promote cross-selling or to devise and promote combinations of products and services.

6.3.2.2 Clustering The term cluster refers to a homogeneous subgroup existing within a population. Clustering techniques are therefore aimed at segmenting a heterogeneous population into a given number of subgroups composed of observations that share similar characteristics; observations included in different clusters have distinctive features. Unlike classification, in clustering there are no predefined classes or reference examples indicating the target class, so that the objects are grouped together based on their mutual homogeneity.

> By defining appropriate metrics and the induced notions of distance and similarity between pairs of observations, the purpose of clustering methods is the identification of homogeneous groups of records called *clusters*. With respect to the specific distance selected, the observations belonging to each cluster must be close to one another and far from those included in other clusters.

Sometimes, the identification of clusters represents a preliminary stage in the data mining process, within exploratory data analysis. It may allow homogeneous data to be processed with the most appropriate rules and techniques and the size of the original dataset to be reduced, since the subsequent data mining activities can be developed autonomously on each cluster identified.

6.3.2.3 Description and Visualization The purpose of a data mining process is sometimes to provide a simple and concise representation of the information stored in a large dataset. Although, in contrast to clustering and association rules, descriptive analysis does not pursue any particular grouping or partition of the records in the dataset, an effective and concise description of information is very helpful since it may suggest possible explanations of hidden patterns in the data and lead to a better understanding of the phenomena to which the data refer. Notice that it is not always easy to obtain a meaningful visualization of the data. However, the effort of representation is justified by the remarkable conciseness of the information achieved through a well-designed chart.

6.4 CRISP-DM Methodology

The Cross Industry Standard Process–Data Mining (CRISP-DM) methodology was initiated in 1996 and represents a generalized pattern applicable to any data mining project. CRISP-DM methodology maps from a general CRISP-DM process into a process with a specific application. In essence, the process model describes the life cycle of the data mining process comprising of six basic steps; the model shows phases, the tasks within individual phases, and relations between them. Data mining projects are iterative; once a goal is reached, or new knowledge and insight are discovered that can be useful in one of the previous phases, it is desirable to revisit the earlier phases.

The CRISP-DM process model is constituted of these six phases:

- Business understanding
- Data understanding
- Data preparation
- Modeling
- Model evaluation
- Model deployment

Figure 6.1 shows a schematic of the CRISP-DM methodology.

The CRISP-DM process can be viewed through four hierarchical levels describing the model at four levels of details, from general

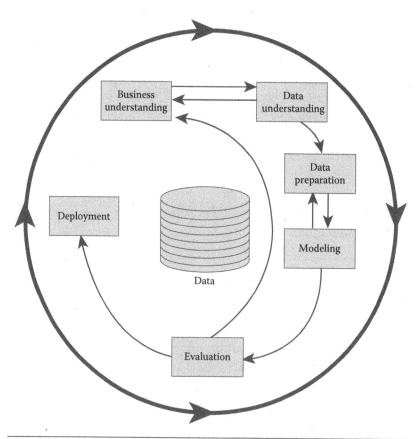

Figure 6.1   Schematic of CRISP-DM methodology.

to specific. Each specific project passes through the phases at the first level; the first level is, at the same time, the most abstract. At the subsequent level, each stage is broken down into generalized, generic tasks. They are generalized as they cover all the possible scenarios in the data mining process, depending on the phase the project is in.

The first level defines the basic phases of the process, that is, the data mining project. The third level defines particular, specialized tasks. They describe how an individual generalized task from the second level is executed in the specific case. For instance, if the second level defines a generic task of data filtering, then the third level describes how this task is executed depending on whether it is a categorical or continuous variable. Finally, the fourth level contains the specific instance of the data mining process, with a range of actions, decisions, and outcomes of the actual knowledge discovery process.

1. Business Understanding

   This phase of the data mining project deals with defining goals and demands from the business point of view. This phase consists of tasks like:
   - Determining business objectives
   - Situation assessment
   - Defining the goals of data mining
   - Producing the project plan

   It determines the problem domain (marketing, user support, or something similar), and also identifies the organization's business units involved with the project. It also identifies the resources required for this project including the hardware and tools for implementation, as well as the human resources, especially the domain-specific experts required for the project.

   At the end of the first phase, a project plan is developed with a list of phases, with constituting tasks and activities, as well as the time and effort estimations; resources for tasks, their interdependencies, inputs, and outputs are also defined. The project plan highlights strategies for issues like risk assessment and quality management.

2. Data Understanding

   This phase of the data mining project deals with getting familiarized with the organization's data through exploratory data analysis, which includes simple statistical characteristics and more complex analyses, that is, applying certain hypotheses to the business problem.

This phase consists of tasks like:

- Collecting initial data
- Describing data
- Exploring data
- Verifying data quality

The data are obtained from identified sources, and the selection criteria are chosen in light of the specific business problem under consideration. Tables are defined, and if the data source is a relational database or a data warehouse, variations of the tables to be used are also specified.

This is followed by analyzing the basic characteristics of the data, such as quantity and types (e.g., categorical or continuous), then analysis of the correlations between variables, the distribution and intervals of values, as well as other simple statistical functions coupled with specialized statistical analysis tools if necessary. It is important to establish the meaning for every variable, especially from the business aspect, and relevance to the specific data mining problem.

The more complex analysis of the dataset entails using one of the online analytical processing (OLAP) or similar visualization tools. This analysis enables shaping of the relevant hypotheses and transforming them into the corresponding mining problem space. In addition, project goals get fine-tuned more precisely.

At the end of this phase, the quality of the dataset is ascertained in terms of the completeness and accuracy of data, the frequency of discrepancies, or the occurrences of the null values.

3. Data Preparation

This phase of the data mining project deals with data preparation for the mining process. It includes choosing the initial dataset on which modeling is to begin, that is, the model set.

This phase consists of tasks like:

- Data selection
- Data cleaning

- Data construction
- Data integration
- Data formatting

When defining the set for the subsequent modeling step, one must take into account, among other things, elimination of individual variables based on the results of statistical tests of correlation and significance, that is, values of individual variables. Taking these into account, the number of variables for the subsequence modeling iteration is reduced, with the aim of obtaining an optimum model. Besides this, this is the phase when the sampling (i.e., reducing the size of the initial dataset) technique is decided on.

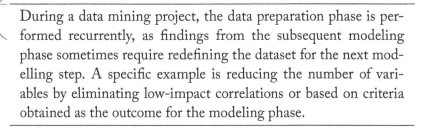

During a data mining project, the data preparation phase is performed recurrently, as findings from the subsequent modeling phase sometimes require redefining the dataset for the next modelling step. A specific example is reducing the number of variables by eliminating low-impact correlations or based on criteria obtained as the outcome for the modeling phase.

At the end of this phase, the issue of data quality is addressed, as well as the manner in which nonexistent values will be managed, as also the strategy for handling particular values. New variables are derived, the values of the existing ones are transformed, and values from different tables are combined in order to obtain new variables values. Finally, individual variables are syntactically adjusted in sync with the modeling tools, without changing their meaning.

4. Modeling

This phase of the data mining project deals with choosing the data mining technique itself. The choice of the tool, that is, the technique to be applied, depends on the nature of the problem. In fact, various techniques can always be applied on the same type of problem, but there is always a technique or tool yielding the best results for a specific problem. It is sometimes necessary to model several techniques and algorithms, and then opt for the one yielding the best results. In other words, several models are built in a single iteration of the phase, and the best one is selected.

This phase consists of tasks like:

- Generating test design
- Building the model
- Assessing the model

Before modeling starts, the data (model) set from the previous phase must be divided into subsets for training, testing, and evaluation. The evaluation subset is used for assessing the model's efficiency on unfamiliar data, whereas the test subset is used for achieving model generality, that is, avoiding the overfitting on the training subset.

Division of the data subset is followed by model building. The effectiveness of the obtained model is assessed on the evaluation subset. In the case of predictive models, applying the obtained model on the evaluation subset produces data for the cumulative gains chart showing how well the model predicts on an unfamiliar set. Parameters for the subsequent modeling step are determined based on the obtained graph, the model quality ratio (surface below the graph) and other ratios, such as significance and value factors for individual variables, and correlations between them. If necessary, the developer returns to the previous phase to eliminate noise variables from the model set.

If several models were built in this phase (even those done using different techniques), then models are compared, and the best ones are selected for the next iteration of the modeling phase. Each obtained model is interpreted from the business point of view, as much as it is possible in the current phase iteration itself.

At the end of this phase, the developers assess the possibility of model deployment, result reliability, and whether the set goals are met from the business and analytic point of view. The modeling phase is repeated until the best, that is, a satisfactory model is obtained.

5. Model Evaluation

This phase of the data mining project deals with the assessment of the final model, that is, the extent to which it meets the goals set in the first phase of the data mining project. The evaluation of the model in the previous phase is more related to the model's technical characteristics (efficiency and generality).

This phase consists of tasks like:
- Evaluating results
- Reviewing the process
- Determining next steps

If the information gained at this point affects the quality of the entire project, this would indicate returning to the first phase and reinitiating the whole process with the newer information. However, if the model meets all the business goals and is considered satisfactory for deployment, a detailed review of the entire data mining process is conducted in order to ascertain the quality of the entire process.

At the end of this phase, the project manager decides on moving to the phase of model deployment or repeating the prior process for improvement.

6. Model Deployment

This phase of the data mining project deals with model deployment in business, taking into account the way of measuring the model's benefits and its fine-tuning on an ongoing basis.

This phase consists of tasks like:
- Preparing a deployment plan
- Monitoring the plan
- Maintenance
- Producing a final report
- Project review

Because of the changing market conditions and competition, it is necessary to repeat the modeling process periodically to fine-tune or alter the model to sustain the effectiveness of the insights drawn from data mining.

The application of the model in strategic decision-making of a business organization can be used for direct measurement of the benefits of the obtained model, and to gather new knowledge for the subsequent iterations for model improvement.

At the end of this phase, the project is concluded by over-all review, that is, analysis of its strengths and weaknesses. Final reports and presentations are made. Documentation with the recording of experiences usable in possible future projects is also compiled.

6.5 Summary

This chapter discussed the basics of data mining. It introduced the concept of data mining with its benefits and applications. After describing details of a data mining analysis, it provided an overview of the CRISP-DM data mining methodology.

7

ANALYTICS SYSTEMS

7.1 Analytics

With recent technological advances and the reduced costs of collecting, transferring, and storing digital information, companies are accumulating increasingly larger repositories of emails, documents, customer loyalty transactions, sensor data, financial information, Internet footprints, and so on.

The combination of intuition and domain knowledge has and will always be instrumental in driving businesses decisions; intuition and instinct are still the most commonly used bases for important and sometimes critical decisions by senior executives and managers. Intuition-based decision-making is prone to serious inaccuracies and errors, while data-backed decision-making, being immune to such failings, is much more powerful. Data hold the promise of providing more accurate documentation of the past. Such objective documentation is necessary for improving awareness, enhancing understanding, and detecting unusual events in the past. Armed with a better understanding of the past, there is a better chance of improving decision-making in the future.

Analytics can be used for improving performance, driving sustainable growth through innovation, speeding up response time to market and environmental changes, and anticipating and planning for change while managing and balancing risk. These benefits are achieved through a framework that deploys automated data analysis within the business context. The paradigm shift is from intuition-driven decision-making to data-driven, computer-assisted decision-making that takes advantage of large amounts of data or data from multiple sources.

Generating insights from data requires transforming the data in its raw form into information that is comprehensible to humans. Humans excel in detecting patterns in data when the data are provided in a manageable size. For example, a domain expert may be able to uncover a trend or pattern in a spreadsheet that includes information on several hundreds of consumers' shop card transactions with a dozen columns of measurements. Even with small samples, it is often difficult for humans to detect patterns and to distinguish real patterns from random ones. However, in the more typical scenario of thousands to millions of customers (rows) and hundreds to thousands of measurements (columns), human experts, no matter how much domain expertise and experience they possess, do not have the capacity to extract patterns or insights from such large amounts of data without the aid of analytics software and knowledge.

Analytics can be defined as the skills, technologies, applications, and practices required for continuous iterative exploration and investigation of past business performance, based on data and statistical methods, to gain insight and drive business planning for the future.

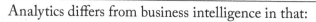

Analytics differs from business intelligence in that:

- Analytics provide system-generated intelligence based on automated data analysis.
- Analytics loops the output assessment back into the business process and system enabling the measurement and further fine tuning of the business benefits.
- Analytics, unlike traditional business intelligence (BI), does not employ a consistent set of metrics to both measure past performance and guide business planning for the future.

7.1.1 Descriptive Analytics

Descriptive analytics summarizes and describes what happened in the past. It includes the various forms of reporting—standard or ad hoc reports, queries, scorecards, alerts. It simply describe what has happened in the past. It may also be used to classify customers or other business entities into groups that are similar on certain dimensions.

7.1.2 Predictive Analytics

Predictive analytics predicts what will happen in the future. Predictive analytics models are very popular in predicting the behavior of customers based on past buying history and perhaps some demographic variables. They typically use multiple variables to predict a particular dependent variable. Examples include using various measures of growing season rainfall and temperatures to predict the price of Bordeaux wine, or using variables about your credit history to predict the likelihood that you will repay loans in the future.

7.1.3 Prescriptive Analytics

Prescriptive analytics determine actions to be taken to make the future happen. Randomized testing, in which a test group is compared to a control group with random assignment of subjects to each group, is a powerful method to establish cause. On comparison of the groups, if one is better than the other with statistical significance, the thing that is being tested in the test group should be prescribed. Optimization is another form of prescriptive analytics. Based on a statistical model, it prescribes what the optimum level of key variables is for maximizing a particular outcome variable. For instance, for maximizing profitability, pricing optimization prescribes the price to charge for your products and services.

7.2 Data Science Techniques

Doing data science means implementing flexible, scalable, and extensible systems for data preparation, analysis, visualization, and modeling.

Many firms are moving away from internally owned, centralized computing systems and toward distributed cloud-based services. Distributed hardware and software systems, including database systems, can be expanded more easily as the data management needs of organizations grow. Utilizing data science means being able to gather data from the full range of database systems, relational and nonrelational, commercial and open source. We employ database query and analysis tools, gathering information across distributed systems, collating information, creating contingency tables and computing indices of relationship across variables of interest. We use information technology and database systems as far as they can take us, and then we do more, applying what we know about statistical inference and the modeling techniques of predictive analytics.

7.2.1 Database Systems

Relational databases have a row-and-column table structure, similar to a spreadsheet. We access and manipulate these data using Structured Query Language (SQL). Because they are transaction-oriented with enforced data integrity, relational databases provide the foundation for sales order processing and financial accounting systems.

Nonrelational databases focus on availability and scalability. They may employ key-value, column-oriented, document-oriented, or graph structures. Some are designed for online or real-time applications, where fast response times are key. Others are well suited for massive storage and off-line analysis, with MapReduce providing a key data aggregation tool.

7.2.2 Statistical Inference

Statistics are functions of sample data and are more credible when samples are representative of the concerned population. Typically, large random samples, small standard errors and narrow confidence intervals are preferred. Formal scientific method suggests that we construct theories and test those theories with sample data. The process involves drawing statistical inferences as point estimates, interval estimates, or tests of hypotheses about the population. Whatever the form of inference, we need sample data relating to questions of interest.

Classical and Bayesian statistics represent alternative approaches to inference, alternative ways of measuring uncertainty about the world.

1. Classical hypothesis testing involves making null hypotheses about population parameters and then rejecting or not rejecting those hypotheses based on sample data. Typical null hypotheses (as the word null would imply) states that there is no difference between proportions or groups, or no relationship between variables.

    To test a null hypothesis, we compute a special statistic called a test statistic along with its associated p-value. Assuming that the null hypothesis is true, we can derive the theoretical distribution of the test statistic. We obtain a p-value by referring the sample test statistic to this theoretical distribution. The p-value, itself a sample statistic, gives the probability of rejecting the null hypothesis under the assumption that it is true. Let us assume that the conditions for valid inference have been satisfied. Then, when we observe a very low p-value (0.05, 0.01, or 0.001, for instance), this indicates that either of these two things must be true:

- An event of very low probability has occurred under the assumption that the null hypothesis is true.
- The null hypothesis is false.

  A low p-value leads us to reject the null hypothesis, and we say the research results are statistically significant. Some results are statistically significant and meaningful.

2. The Bayesian approach treats parameters as random variables having probability distributions representing of our uncertainty about the world which can be reduced by collecting relevant sample data. Sample data and Bayes' theorem are used to derive posterior probability distributions for these same parameters, which in turn are used to obtain conditional probabilities.

7.2.3 Regression and Classification

Data science involves a search for meaningful relationships between variables. We look for relationships between pairs of continuous variables using scatter plots and correlation coefficients. We look for relationships between categorical variables using contingency tables and the methods of categorical data analysis. We use multivariate methods and multi-way contingency tables to examine relationships among many variables. There are two main types of predictive models: regression and classification. Regression is prediction of a response of meaningful magnitude. Classification involves prediction of a class or category.

The most common form of regression is least-squares regression, also called ordinary least-squares regression, linear regression, or multiple regression. When we use ordinary least-squares regression, we estimate regression coefficients so that they minimize the sum of the squared residuals, where residuals are differences between the observed and predicted response values. For regression problems, we think of the response as taking any value along the real number line, although in practice the response may take a limited number of distinct values. The important thing for regression is that the response values have meaningful magnitude.

Poisson regression is useful for counts. The response has meaningful magnitude but takes discrete (whole number) values with a minimum value of zero. Log-linear models for frequencies, grouped frequencies, and contingency tables for cross-classified observations fall within this domain.

Most traditional modeling techniques involve linear models or linear equations. The response or transformed response is on the left-hand side of the linear model. The linear predictor is on the right-hand side. The linear predictor involves explanatory variables and is linear in its parameters, that is, it involves the addition of coefficients or the multiplication of coefficients by the explanatory variables. The coefficients we fit to linear models represent estimates of population parameters.

Generalized linear models, as their name would imply, are generalizations of the classical linear regression model. They include models for choices and counts, including logistic regression, multinomial logit models, log-linear models, ordinal logistic models, Poisson regression, and survival data models. To introduce the theory behind these important models, we begin by reviewing the classical linear regression model. Generalized linear models help us model what are obvious nonlinear relationships between explanatory variables and responses.

Linear regression is a special generalized linear model. It has normally distributed responses and an identity link relating the expected value of responses to the linear predictor. Linear regression coefficients may be estimated by ordinary least squares. For other members of the family of generalized linear models, we use maximum likelihood estimation. With the classical linear model, we have analysis of variance and F-tests. With generalized linear models, we have analysis of deviance and likelihood ratio tests, which are asymptotic chi-square tests.

The method of logistic regression, although called "regression," is actually a classification method. It involves the prediction of a binary response. Ordinal and multinomial logit models extend logistic regression to problems involving more than two classes. Linear discriminant analysis is another classification method from the domain of traditional statistics.

7.2.4 Data Mining and Machine Learning

Machine learning refers to the methods or algorithms that are used as an alternative to traditional statistical methods. When we apply these methods in the analysis of data, it is termed *data mining*. Recommender systems, collaborative filtering, association rules, optimization methods based on heuristics, as well as a myriad of methods for regression, classification, and clustering, are all examples of machine learning. With traditional statistics, we define the model specification prior to working with the data and also make assumptions about the population distributions from which the data have been drawn. Machine learning, on the other hand, is data-adaptive: model specification is defined by applying algorithms to the data. With machine learning, a few assumptions are made about the underlying distributions of the data.

Cluster analysis is referred to as unsupervised learning to distinguish it from classification, which is supervised learning, guided by known, coded values of a response variable or class. Association rules modeling, frequent itemsets, social network analysis, link analysis, recommender systems, and many multivariate methods employed in data science represent unsupervised learning methods.

An important multivariate method, principal component analysis, draws on linear algebra and provides a way to reduce the number of measures or quantitative features we use to describe domains of interest. Long a staple of measurement experts and a prerequisite of *factor analysis*, principal component analysis has seen recent applications in *latent semantic analysis*—a technology for identifying important topics across a corpus of documents.

7.2.5 Data Visualization

Statistical summaries fail to tell the story of data. To understand data, we must look beyond data tables, regression coefficients, and the results of statistical tests. Visualization tools help us learn from data. We explore data, discover patterns in data, and identify groups of observations that go together and unusual observations or outliers. Data visualization is critical to the work of data science in the areas of discovery (exploratory data analysis), diagnostics (statistical modeling), and design (presentation graphics).

R is particularly strong in data visualization.

7.2.6 Text Analytics

Text analytics is an important and growing area of predictive analytics. Text analytics draws from a variety of disciplines, including linguistics, communication and language arts, experimental psychology, political discourse analysis, journalism, computer science, and statistics.

The output from these processes such as crawling, scraping, and parsing is a document collection or text corpus in the natural language. The two primary ways of analyzing a text corpus are the *bag of words* approach and *natural language processing*. We parse the corpus further, creating commonly formatted expressions, indices, keys, and matrices that are more easily analyzed by computer. This additional parsing is sometimes referred to as text annotation. We extract features from the text and then use those features in subsequent analyses. Natural language processing is more than a collection of individual words: natural language conveys meaning.

Natural language documents contain paragraphs, paragraphs contain sentences, and sentences contain words. There are grammatical rules, with many ways to convey the same idea, along with exceptions to rules and rules about exceptions. Words used in combination and the rules of grammar comprise the linguistic foundations of text analytics. Linguists study natural language, the words and the rules that we use to form meaningful utterances. "Generative grammar" is a general term for the rules; "morphology," "syntax," and "semantics" are more specific terms. Computer programs for natural language processing use linguistic rules to mimic human communication and convert natural language into structured text for further analysis.

A key step in text analysis is the creation of a terms-by-documents matrix (sometimes called a lexical table). The rows of this data matrix correspond to words or word stems from the document collection, and the columns correspond to documents in the collection. The entry in each cell of a terms-by-documents matrix could be a binary indicator for the presence or absence of a term in a document, a frequency count of the number of times a term is used in a document, or a weighted frequency indicating the importance of a term in a document. After being created, the terms-by-documents matrix is like an index, a mapping of document identifiers to terms (keywords or stems) and vice versa.

For information retrieval systems or search engines we might also retain information regarding the specific location of terms within documents.

An alternative system might distinguish among parts of speech, permitting more sophisticated syntactic searches across documents.

Typical text analytics applications:

1. Spam filtering has long been a subject of interest as a classification problem, and many email users have benefited from the efficient algorithms that have evolved in this area. In the context of information retrieval, search engines classify documents as being relevant to the search or not. Useful modeling techniques for text classification include logistic regression, linear discriminant function analysis, classification trees, and support vector machines. Various ensemble or committee methods may be employed.

2. Automatic text summarization is an area of research and development that can help with information management. Imagine a text processing program with the ability to read each document in a collection and summarize it in a sentence or two, perhaps quoting from the document itself. Today's search engines are providing partial analysis of documents prior to their being displayed. They create automated summaries for fast information retrieval. They recognize common text strings associated with user requests. These applications of text analysis comprise tools of information search that we take for granted as part of our daily lives.

3. Sentiment analysis is measurement-focused text analysis. Sometimes called opinion mining, one approach to sentiment analysis is to draw on positive and negative word sets (lexicons, dictionaries) that convey human emotion or feeling. These word sets are specific to the language being spoken and the context of application. Another approach to sentiment analysis is to work directly with text samples and human ratings of

those samples, developing text scoring methods specific to the task at hand. The objective of sentiment analysis is to score text for affect, feelings, attitudes, or opinions. Sentiment analysis and text measurement in general hold promise as technologies for understanding consumer opinion and markets. Just as political researchers can learn from the words of the public, press, and politicians, business researchers can learn from the words of customers and competitors. There are customer service logs, telephone transcripts, and sales call reports, along with user group, Listserv, and blog postings. And we have ubiquitous social media from which to build document collections for text and sentiment analysis.

4. Text measures flow from a measurement model (algorithms for scoring) and a dictionary, both defined by the researcher or analyst. A dictionary in this context is not a traditional dictionary; it is not an alphabetized list of words and their definitions. Rather, the dictionary used to construct text measures is a repository of word lists, such as synonyms and antonyms, positive and negative words, strong and weak sounding words, bipolar adjectives, parts of speech, and so on. The lists come from expert judgments about the meaning of words. A text measure assigns numbers to documents according to rules, with the rules being defined by the word lists, scoring algorithms, and modeling techniques in predictive analytics.

7.2.7 Time Series and Market Research Models

Sales and marketing data are organized by observational unit, time, and space. The observational unit is typically an economic agent (individual or firm) or a group of such agents as in an aggregate analysis. It is common to use geographical areas as a basis for aggregation. Alternatively, space (longitude and latitude) can be used directly in spatial data analyses. Time considerations are especially important in macroeconomic analysis, which focuses upon nationwide economic measures.

The term time series regression refers to regression analysis in which the organizing unit of analysis is time. We look at relationships among economic measures organized in time. Much economic analysis concerns time series regression. Special care must be taken to avoid what might be called spurious relationships, as many economic time series are correlated with one another because they depend upon underlying factors, such as population growth or seasonality. In time series regression, we use standard linear regression methods. We check the residuals from our regression to ensure that they are not correlated in time. If they are correlated in time (autocorrelated), then we use a method such as generalized least squares as an alternative to ordinary least squares, that is, we incorporate an error data model as part of our modeling process. Longitudinal data analysis or panel data analysis is an example of a mixed data method with a focus on data organized by cross-sectional units and time.

Sales forecasts can build on the special structure of sales data as they are found in business. These are data organized by time and location, where location might refer to geographical regions or sales territories, stores, departments within stores, or product lines. Sales forecasts are a critical component of business planning and a first step in the budgeting process. Models and methods that provide accurate forecasts can be of great benefit to management. They help managers to understand the determinants of sales, including promotions, pricing, advertising, and distribution. They reveal competitive position and market share. There are many approaches to forecasting. Some are judgmental, relying on expert opinion or consensus. There are top-down and bottom-up forecasts, and various techniques for combining the views of experts. Other approaches depend on the analysis of past sales data.

1. Forecasting by time periods: These may be days, weeks, months, or whatever intervals make sense for the problem at hand. Time dependencies can be noted in the same manner as in traditional time-series models. Autoregressive terms are useful in many contexts. Time-construed covariates, such as day of the week or month of the year, can be added to provide additional predictive power. An analyst can work with time series data, using past sales to predict future sales, noting overall trends and cyclical patterns in the data. Exponential smoothing, moving averages, and various regression and econometric methods may be used with time-series data.
2. Forecasting by location: Organizing data by location contributes to a model's predictive power. Location may itself be used

as a factor in models. In addition, we can search for explanatory variables tied to location. With geographical regions, for example, we might include consumer and business demographic variables known to relate to sales.

Sales dollars per time period is the typical response variable of interest in sales forecasting studies. Alternative response variables include sales volume and time to sale. Related studies of market share require information about the sales of other firms in the same product category.

When we use the term time series analysis, however, we are not talking about time series regression. We are talking about methods that start by focusing on one economic measure at a time and its pattern across time. We look for trends, seasonality, and cycles in that individual time series. Then, after working with that single time series, we look at possible relationships with other time series. If we are concerned with forecasting or predicting the future, as we often are in predictive analytics, then we use methods of time series analysis. Recently, there has been considerable interest in state space models for time series, which provide a convenient mechanism for incorporating regression components into dynamic time series models.

There are myriad applications of time series analysis in marketing, including marketing mix models and advertising research models. Along with sales forecasting, these fall under the general class of market response models. Marketing mix models look at the effects of price, promotion, and product placement in retail establishments. These are multiple time series problems. Advertising research looks for the cumulative effectiveness of advertising on brand and product awareness, as well as sales.

Much of this research employs defined measures such as "advertising stock," which attempt to convert advertising impressions or rating points to a single measure in time. The thinking is that messages are most influential immediately after being received, decline in influence with time, but do not decline completely until many units in time later. Viewers or listeners remember advertisements long after initial exposure to those advertisements. Another way of saying this is to note that there is a carry-over effect from one time period to the next. Needless to say, measurement and modeling on the subject of advertising effectiveness presents many challenges for the marketing data scientist.

7.3 Snapshot of Data Analysis Techniques and Tasks

There is no universally accepted best data analysis method; choosing particular data analytic tool(s) or some combination with traditional methods is entirely dependent on the particular application, and it requires human interaction to decide on the suitability of a blended approach. Depending on the desired outcome, several data analysis techniques with different goals may be applied successively to achieve a desired result. For example, to determine which customers are likely to buy a new product, a business analyst may need first to use cluster analysis to segment the customer database, then apply regression analysis to predict buying behavior for each cluster.

Table 7.1 presents a selection of analysis techniques and tasks.

A useful selection of data analysis techniques:

1. Descriptive and Visualization techniques include simple descriptive statistics such as:
   - Averages and measures of variation
   - Counts and percentages
   - Cross-tabs and simple correlations

Table 7.1 Analysis Techniques versus Tasks

DATA ANALYSIS TECHNIQUES	DATA SUMMARIZATION	SEGMENTATION	CLASSIFICATION	PREDICTION	DEPENDENCY ANALYSIS
Descriptive and visualization	◆	◆			◆
Correlation analysis					◆
Cluster analysis		◆			
Discriminant analysis			◆		
Regression analysis				◆	◆
Neural networks		◆	◆	◆	
Case-based reasoning					◆
Decision trees			◆	◆	
Association rules					◆

They are useful for understanding the structure of the data. Visualization is primarily a discovery technique and is useful for interpreting large amounts of data; visualization tools include histograms, box plots, scatter diagrams, and multi-dimensional surface plots

2. Correlation Analysis measures the relationship between two variables. The resulting correlation coefficient shows if changes in one variable will result in changes in the other. When comparing the correlation between two variables, the goal is to see if a change in the independent variable will result in a change in the dependent variable. This information helps in understanding an independent variable's predictive abilities. Correlation findings, just as regression findings, can be useful in analyzing causal relationships, but they do not by themselves establish causal patterns.

3. Cluster Analysis seeks to organize information about variables so that relatively homogeneous groups, or "clusters," can be formed. The clusters formed with this family of methods should be highly internally homogenous (members are similar to one another) and highly externally heterogeneous (members are not like members of other clusters)

4. Discriminant Analysis is used to predict membership in two or more mutually exclusive groups from a set of predictors, when there is no natural ordering on the groups. Discriminant analysis can be seen as the inverse of a one-way multivariate analysis of variance (MANOVA) in that the levels of the independent variable (or factor) for MANOVA become the categories of the dependent variable for discriminant analysis, and the dependent variables of the MANOVA become the predictors for discriminant analysis.

5. Regression Analysis is a statistical tool that uses the relation between two or more quantitative variables so that one variable (the dependent variable) can be predicted from the other(s) (independent variables). But no matter how strong the statistical relations are between the variables, no cause-and-effect pattern is necessarily implied by the regression model. There are many types of regression analysis,

including simple linear, multiple linear, curvilinear, multiple curvilinear regression models, and logistic regression.

6. Neural Networks (NN) are a class of systems modeled after the human brain. As the human brain consists of millions of neurons that are interconnected by synapses, NN are formed from large numbers of simulated neurons, connected to each other in a manner similar to brain neurons. As in the human brain, the strength of neuron interconnections may change (or be changed by the learning algorithm) in response to a presented stimulus or an obtained output, which enables the network to "learn."

A disadvantage of NN is that building the initial neural network model can be especially time-intensive because input processing almost always means that raw data must be transformed. Variable screening and selection requires large amounts of the analysts' time and skill. Also, for the user without a technical background, figuring out how NN operate is far from obvious.

7. Case-Based Reasoning (CBR) is a technology that tries to solve a given problem by making direct use of past experiences and solutions. A case is usually a specific problem that was encountered and solved previously. Given a particular new problem, CBR examines the set of stored cases and finds similar ones. If similar cases exist, their solution is applied to the new problem, and the problem is added to the case base for future reference.

A disadvantage of CBR is that the solutions included in the case database may not be optimal in any sense because they are limited to what was actually done in the past, not necessarily what should have been done under similar circumstances. Therefore, using them may simply perpetuate earlier mistakes.

8. Decision Trees (DT) are like those used in decision analysis where each nonterminal node represents a test or decision on the data item considered. Depending on the outcome of the test, one chooses a certain branch. To classify a particular data item, one would start at the root node and follow the assertions down until a terminal node (or leaf) is reached;

at that point, a decision is made. DT can also be interpreted as a special form of a rule set, characterized by their hierarchical organization of rules.

A disadvantage of DT is that trees use up data very rapidly in the training process. They should never be used with small datasets. They are also highly sensitive to noise in the data, and they try to fit the data exactly, which is referred to as "overfitting." Overfitting means that the model depends too strongly on the details of the particular dataset used to create it. When a model suffers from overfitting, it is unlikely to be externally valid (i.e., it won't hold up when applied to a new dataset).

9. Association Rules (AR) are statements about relationships between the attributes of a known group of entities and one or more aspects of those entities that enable predictions to be made about aspects of other entities who are not in the group, but who possess the same attributes. More generally, AR state a statistical correlation between the occurrences of certain attributes in a data item, or between certain data items in a dataset. The general form of an AR is $X_1...X_n => Y[C,S]$ which means that the attributes $X_1, ..., X_n$ predict Y with a confidence C and a significance S.

A useful selection of data analysis tasks:

1. Data Summarization gives the user an overview of the structure of the data and is generally carried out in the early stages of a project. This type of initial exploratory data analysis can help to understand the nature of the data and to find potential hypotheses for hidden information. Simple descriptive statistical and visualization techniques generally apply.

2. Segmentation separates the data into interesting and meaningful subgroups or classes. In this case, the analyst can hypothesize certain subgroups as relevant for the business question based on prior knowledge or based on the outcome of data description and summarization. Automatic clustering techniques can detect previously unsuspected and hidden structures in data that allow segmentation. Clustering techniques, visualization, and neural nets generally apply.

3. Classification assumes that a set of objects—characterized by some attributes or features—belong to different classes. The class label is a discrete qualitative identifier; for example, large, medium, or small. The objective is to build classification models that assign the correct class to previously unseen and unlabeled objects. Classification models are mostly used for predictive modeling. Discriminant analysis, decision tree, rule induction methods, and genetic algorithms generally apply.

4. Prediction is very similar to classification. The difference is that in prediction, the class is not a qualitative discrete attribute but a continuous one. The goal of prediction is to find the numerical value of the target attribute for unseen objects; this problem type is also known as regression, and if the prediction deals with time series data, then it is often called forecasting. Regression analysis, decision trees, and neural nets generally apply.

5. Dependency Analysis deals with finding a model that describes significant dependencies (or associations) between data items or events. Dependencies can be used to predict the value of an item given information on other data items. Dependency analysis has close connections with classification and prediction because the dependencies are implicitly used for the formulation of predictive models. Correlation analysis, regression analysis, association rules, case-based reasoning, and visualization techniques generally apply.

7.4 Summary

The chapter presents the basics of analytics which are an essential component of any performance intelligence project. The chapter describes the various kinds of analytics such as descriptive, predictive, and prescriptive analytics. The chapter then provides an overview of the data science and related techniques.

8

BUSINESS INTELLIGENCE SYSTEMS

Business Intelligence (BI) enables enterprises to access current, correct, consistent, and complete information on any process or transaction to take informed decisions in compliance with its strategy, policy, and procedures. Other than the concept and technologies of BI, this chapter introduces the novel concept of decision patterns that consolidate based on ongoing operations and transactions, and then expedite the efficacy of decisions. A BI ecosystem consists of data warehouse management tools, ETL (extraction, transformation, loading), data integration, and BI tools. The main BI activities include query, reporting, online analytical processing (OLAP), statistical analysis, forecasting, data mining, and decision support.

8.1 Concept of Business Intelligence

A number of enterprises have started to view their data as a corporate asset and to realize that properly collecting, aggregating, and analyzing their data opens an opportunity to discover pieces of knowledge that can both automate business decisions in certain well-defined areas of activity, or support business decisions in the context of customary and recurring decision patterns of the past. At the least, they can improve operational processing and provide better insight into customer profiles and behavior. BI is the process of using advanced applications and technologies to gather, store, analyze, and transform overload of business information into actionable knowledge that provides significant business value. The concept of BI has been introduced into the marketplace in order to enhance its ability to make better and more efficient business decisions.

8.2 Business Intelligence

Business Intelligence (BI) can be defined as the techniques, technologies, and tools needed to turn data into information, information into actionable knowledge, and actionable knowledge into execution plans that drive profitable business action. Business intelligence encompasses data warehousing, business analytic tools, and content/knowledge management.

BI involves the infrastructure of managing and presenting data including the hardware platforms, relational or other types of database systems, and associated software tools for governance and compliance. It also incorporates query, processing, and reporting tools that provide informed access to the data. Additionally, BI involves the analytical components, such as online analytical processing (OLAP), data quality, data profiling, predictive analysis, and other types of data mining. Being able to take action based on the intelligence that has been gleaned from BI is the key point of any BI. It is through these actions that a senior management sponsor can see the true return on investment in BI. A BI program provides insights and/or decision support that increases business efficiency, increases sales, provides better customer targeting, reduces customer service costs, identifies fraud, and generally increases profits while reducing corresponding costs.

8.3 Benefits of BI

1. Improving the competitive response and decision-making process.

   To realize a long-lasting competitive advantage, an organization needs to have rapid and continuous innovation and dynamic coupling of processes so that they cannot be easily duplicated. Moreover, firms also need to leverage on resources such as structural capital, human capital, and relationship capital to achieve sustainable competitive advantage. With BI systems connected to customer relationship management, enterprise resource planning, human resource, and finance systems, information can be produced in a more accurate and timely manner. BI systems thus make up a complex solution that allows decision makers to create, aggregate, and share knowledge in an organization easily, along with greatly improved service quality for efficient decision-making.

2. Enhancing the effectiveness of customer relationship management.

   Leveraging BI, customer relationship management (CRM) enhances the relationship between the organization and its customers. With good relationships, customers' loyalty can then be achieved where future sales can be generated. With timely information available for executives and managers to make better and faster decisions, the organization will be able to provide quality service to its customers and respond effectively to changing business conditions. An BI-enabled CRM provides an organization with the ability to categories or segment its existing customer base and prospects more accurately. This may be accomplished based on the products or services that a client purchases, demographic information for consumer clients, industry sector, or company size for corporate clients, and so on. BI-enabled customer relationship management allows an organization to better understand the trend or buying pattern of its existing customers and the segmentation of customer-base would assist sales and marketing to sell products or services (which their customers want) as below:

   a. *Revenue generation via customer profiling and targeted marketing*: Business intelligence reports and analyses reflecting customer transactions and other interactions enable the development of individual customer profiles incorporating demographic, psychographic, and behavioral data about each individual to support customer community segmentation into a variety of clusters based on different attributes and corresponding values. These categories form the basis of sales and profitability measures by customer category, helping to increase sales efforts and customer satisfaction.

   b. *Improved customer satisfaction via profiling, personalization, and customer lifetime value analysis*: Employing the results of customer profiling can do more than just enhance that customer's experience by customizing the presentation of material or content. Customer profiles can be directly integrated into all customer interactions, especially at inbound call centers, where customer profiles can improve a customer service representative's ability to deal with the customer, expedite problem resolution, and perhaps even increase product and service sales. Customer lifetime value analysis calculates the measure of a customer's profitability over the lifetime of the relationship, incorporating the costs associated with managing that relationship as well as the revenues expected from that customer.

c. *Risk management via identification of fraud, abuse, and leakage*: Fraud detection is a type of analysis that looks for prevalent types of patterns that appear with some degree of frequency within certain identified scenarios. Fraud, which includes intentional acts of deception with knowledge that the action or representation could result in an inappropriate gain, rather than being an exception or a work around, is often perpetrated through the exploitation of systemic scenarios. Reporting of the ways that delivered products and services matched with what had been sold to customers (within the contexts of their contracts/ agreements) may highlight areas of revenue leakage. Both of these risks can be analyzed and brought to the attention of the proper internal authorities for remediation.

d. *Improved procurement and acquisition productivity through spend analysis*: Spend analysis incorporates the collection, standardization, and categorization of product purchase and supplier data to select the most dependable vendors, streamline the Request for Proposal (RFP) and procurement process, reduce costs, improve the predictability of high-value supply chains, and improve supply-chain predictability and efficiency.

3. Easing corporate governance and regulatory compliance.
With increased expectations on traceability of data, an organization must be able to verify the lineage of data, starting at their source and tracking them through their various manipulations and aggregations, which in turn means having reliable metadata and data auditing that are consistent across the enterprise.

In this respect, BI assists in ensuring the accuracy of data across the enterprise. It allows reporting and query results to be consistent when they are produced. This is crucial for corporate governance and regulatory compliance when auditing does not find discrepancies in the reports produced.

8.4 Technologies of BI

8.4.1 Data Warehousing and Data Marts

Data warehouses allow sophisticated analysis of large amounts of time-based data, independently of the systems that process the daily transactional data of the enterprise. A data warehouse typically contains time-based summarizations of the underlying detailed transactions; only necessary attributes are extracted from the original source data. Then the data are transformed to conform to the format of the data warehouse and also "cleansed" to ensure quality. In order to create these summary "snapshots," the level of summary detail for the data components must be predefined, and it is fixed for the life of the warehouse, ensuring consistent analysis. This level of summarization is called the granularity of the warehouse. This granularity then determines, for all subsequent data retrieval, the level of transactional detail available for any potential analysis. Aggregating the data reduces the overall number of records necessary to perform specific analyses.

8.4.2 Data Mining

Data mining is of great interest because it is imperative for enterprises to realize the competitive value of the information residing within their data repositories. The goal of data mining is to provide the capability to convert high-volume data into high-value information. This involves discovering patterns of information within large repositories of enterprise data. Enterprises that are most likely to benefit from data mining

1. Exist in competitive markets
2. Have large volumes of data
3. Have communities of information consumers who are not trained as statisticians
4. Have enterprise data that are complex in nature

More traditional Business Intelligence (BI) tools enable users to generate ad hoc reports, business graphics, and test hunches. This is useful for analyzing profitability, product line performance, and so on. Data mining techniques can be applied when users do not already know what they are looking for: data mining provides an automatic method for discovering patterns in data.

Data mining accomplishes two different things:

- It gleans enterprise information from historical data.
- It combines historic enterprise information with current conditions and goals to reduce uncertainty about enterprise outcomes.

Customer-centric data mining techniques can be used to build models of past business experience that can be applied to predict customer behavior and achieve benefits in the future. Data mining provides insights for:

- Learning patterns that allow rapid, proper routing of customer inquiries
- Learning customer buying habits to suggest likely products of interest
- Categorizing customers for focused attention (e.g., churn prediction, prevention)
- Providing predictive models to reduce cost and allow more competitive pricing (e.g., fraud/waste control)
- Assisting purchasers in the selection of inventory of customer-preferred products

8.4.3 Online Analytical Process

Online Analytical Process (OLAP) accommodates queries that would otherwise have been computationally impossible on a relational database management system. OLAP technology is characterized by multidimensionality, and the concept represents one of its key features. Generally, OLAP involves many data items in complex relationships. Its objectives are to analyze these relationships and look for patterns, trends, exceptions, and to answer queries. It is necessary to note that the whole process of OLAP must be carried out online with a rapid response time to provide just-in-time information for effective decision-making. OLAP operations typically include rollup (increasing the level of aggregation) and drill-down (decreasing the level of aggregation or increasing the details) along with one or more dimension hierarchies, slice and dice (selection and projection), and pivot (reorienting the multidimensional view of data). For instance, it allows users to analyze data such as revenue from any dimension such as region or product line anytime of the year. The ability to present data in different perspectives involves complex calculations between data elements, and thus enables users to pursue an analytical process without being thwarted by the system.

8.4.4 Business Intelligence

Operational enterprise systems are designed to support traditional reporting requirements such as day books, party (customer and supplier) ledgers, balance sheets, income statements, and cash flow statements. Data are captured and maintained at the transaction level and later summarized for specific reporting periods. Enterprise data requirements also tend to be relatively short term, again to support the most recent statement reporting. Once the data have been processed and the accounting period closed, the data are archived.

On the other hand, business intelligence information is structured to provide real-time data that are essential in current decision-making processes. The transactional data collected by traditional enterprise information systems are useful but are not the only source of data for business intelligence. In today's enterprises, data collection goes beyond the enterprise data, and it is often stored in distributed and heterogeneous environments. Consequently, business intelligence requirements create significant data storage and manipulation problems that are not encountered in standard enterprise reporting. Furthermore, the short-term availability of data for enterprise requirements, because of its periodic archival, is in contrast to the data needs of business intelligence, which tend to require data for longer time periods (e.g., to support trending and comparative analysis) as well as the need for complex modeling processes. To create useful information, the enterprise data must be aggregated and supplemented by data from other sources that describe the organizational environment.

> The fundamental difference between data warehouse and business intelligence is the data requirements and the need to manipulate them in order to provide alternative views of the data. Typically, enterprise requirements center around repetitive time-based aggregations, whereas business intelligence needs are more dynamic and require sophisticated models.

A major challenge in designing a business intelligence system stems from the relationship between the detailed operational and the aggregated data warehouse systems. The data warehouse model creates a design and implementation situation where the supply of data has been predefined (legacy enterprise systems, other internal data collection systems, and external data repositories), but the user requirements have not been defined. User requirements tend to be ambiguous and require significant flexibility to respond to changing competitive requirements (unlike standard enterprise reporting). To address this problem of incongruent levels of granularity among systems, data marts have been employed. A data mart is a more limited data collection, designed to address the needs of specific users, as opposed to the more general audience of the warehouse. The data mart, however, still draws data from the general data warehouse and consequently is still governed by the granularity and scope restrictions dictated for the warehouse. Figure 8.1 shows the general relationship among operational data, data warehouses, and data marts.

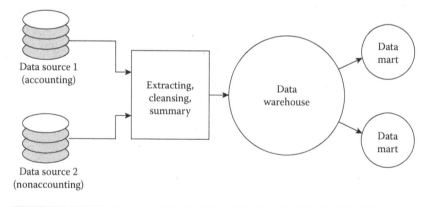

Figure 8.1   Relationship among operational data, data warehouse, and data marts.

8.5 Applications of BI

BI is thus applicable to various industries such as communications, education, financial services, government and public sectors, consumer product goods, healthcare, pharmaceuticals, retail, technology, manufacturing, etc., for the purposes of improving productivity and enhancing decision-making.

1. Banking and Financial Services

   BI has been applied in the banking and financial services industry to perform customer risk analysis and customer valuation on issues such as current profitability, lifetime potential of a customer based on costs, revenue, and future predictive behavior, among others. BI has the ability to do profiling by identifying like-minded customers, thus enabling more accurate segmentation. It also has the ability to create, refine, and target campaigns to win profitable new customers. With these capabilities intertwined with CRM effort, banking and financial institutions are able to effectively serve their customers and gain deeper customer insight. In addition, BI automates compliance with reporting standards and regulations which are crucial to these institutions to improve control and productivity.

2. Pharmaceuticals and Life Sciences

   BI has been applied in the pharmaceuticals and life sciences services industry to identify products that yield better results with a clinical trial research process that segments, tracks, analyses, and shares test results. The systems can also analyze and report on clinical performance data to identify best practices and decide whether to continue, pursue, or terminate a project. BI enables optimizing the supply chain by sharing production information with suppliers, tracking product quality, optimizing stock replenishment, and monitoring vendor performance. Similarly, BI optimizes campaign creation and implementation by analyzing the effectiveness of marketing strategies, and increases sales productivity by understanding the sales activities, territory, and representative performances. BI enhances operational, sales, and marketing performance and enables better compliance with regulatory requirements.

3. Retail

   BI has been applied to improve purchasing, forecasting, and distribution management. BI systems help retailers to optimize product profitability and increase the effectiveness of marketing campaigns, identify and segment customers to enable retention strategies, integrate management and financial reporting for improved performance, and reduce and control operational costs through optimized store performance and effective customer service. BI is able to help in increasing profit margins by aligning corporate and store operations around critical revenue and profitable targets; providing sales and item movement information to operations, marketing, and merchandising; improving customer satisfaction by identifying trends and responding to customer buying needs and behavior; and optimizing profitability by planning and adjusting resources accordingly. Firms are able to improve store performance by improving visibility and accountability for top controllable expenses like labor and cost of goods sold; by communicating sales and margin information across the chain with enterprise-scale reporting, through identification of high- or low-performing divisions, stores, channels, products, and staff; by optimizing staffing levels through headcount planning and workforce analytics; and by monitoring turnover, customer satisfaction, returns, sales trends, and employee utilization through retail scorecards.

4. Manufacturing

   BI has been applied to improve sales performance, increase profitability, improve operational effectiveness, and optimize the supply chain. BI has been applied in the manufacturing industry to analyze cost components and drivers, in order to reduce the cost of goods sold. BI is also able to gain visibility into demand and sales trends in order to optimize investments in inventory. With BI systems, manufacturing companies can identify and analyze excess, obsolete, or slow-moving inventory that can be scrapped or repurposed. The companies can also receive timely notification of events such as late supplier delivery, changes in customer demand, or production stoppages. With the help of BI and integration with CRM, Supply Chain Management (SCM), and Product Lifecycle Management (PLM) effort, these companies are able to respond quickly to changing markets and company sensitivities.

8.6 Summary

This chapter introduced the concept of Business Intelligence (BI), technologies, and applications. It explained how BI enables enterprises to take informed decisions in compliance with their strategy, policy, and procedures.

PART III
PERFORMANCE INTELLIGENCE

9
DECISION PATTERNS

Architectural patterns capture the essential properties required for the successful design of a certain building area or function while leaving large degrees of freedom to architects. The pattern-based approach has also been used in IT to capture best practices of how applications and systems of applications should be designed. This chapter introduces the concept of patterns as a precursor to its employment for performance decision patterns in the next chapter.

9.1 Concept of Patterns

The concept of patterns used in this book originated from the area of real architecture. C. Alexander gathered architectural knowledge and best practices regarding building structures in a pattern format. This knowledge was obtained from years of practical experience. A pattern according to Alexander is structured text that follows a well-defined format and captures nuggets of advice on how to deal with recurring problems in a specific domain. It advises the architect on how to create building architecture, defines the important design decisions, and covers limitations to consider. Patterns can be very generic documents, but may also include concrete measurements and plans. Their application to a certain problem is, however, always a manual task that is performed by the architect. Therefore, each application of a pattern will result in a different looking building, but all applications of the pattern will share a common set of desired properties. For instance, there are patterns describing how eating tables should be sized so that people can move around the table freely, get seated comfortably, find enough room for plates and food, while still being able to communicate and talk during meals without feeling too distant from people seated across the table. While the properties of the table are easy to enforce once concrete distances and sizes are specified, they are extremely hard to determine theoretically or by pure computation using a building's blueprint.

In building architecture, pattern-based descriptions of best practices and design decisions proved especially useful, because many desirable properties of houses, public environments, cities, streets, etc. are not formally measurable. They are perceived by humans and, thus, cannot be computed or predicted in a formal way. Therefore, best practices and well-perceived architectural styles capture a lot of implicit knowledge how people using and living in buildings perceive their structure, functionality, and the general feel. Especially, the different emotions that buildings trigger, such as awe and feelings of comfort, coziness, power, and cleanness are hard to measure or explain and are also referred to as "the quality without a name" or the inner beauty of a building. How certain objectives can be realized in architecture is, thus, found only through practical experience, which is then captured by patterns. For example, there are patterns describing how lighting in a room should be realized so that people feel comfortable and positive. Architects capture their knowledge gathered from existing buildings and feedback they received from users in patterns describing well-perceived building design. In this regard, each pattern describes one architectural solution for an architectural problem. It does so in an abstract format that allows for implementation in various ways. Architectural patterns, thus, capture the essential properties required for the successful design of a certain building area or function while leaving large degrees of freedom to architects.

Multiple patterns are connected and inter related resulting in a pattern language. This concept of links between patterns is used to point to related patterns. For example, an architect reviewing patterns describing different roof types can be pointed to patterns describing different solutions for windows in these roofs and may be advised that some window solutions, thus, the patterns describing them, cannot be combined with a certain roof pattern. For example, a flat rooftop cannot be combined with windows that have to be mounted vertically. Also, a pattern language uses these links to guide an architect through the design of buildings, streets, cities, etc. by describing the order in which patterns have to be considered. For example, the size of the ground on which a building is created may limit the general architecture patterns that should be selected first. After this, the number of floors can be considered, the above mentioned roofing style, etc.

1. Patterns in Information Technology (IT) Solutions

   In a similar way, the pattern-based approach has been used in IT to capture best practices as to how applications and systems of applications should be designed. Examples are patterns for fault-tolerant software, general application architecture, object-oriented programming, enterprise applications, or for message-based application integration. Again, these patterns are abstract and independent of the programming language or runtime infrastructure used to form timeless knowledge that can be applied in various IT environments. In the domain of IT solutions, the desirable properties are portability, manageability, flexibility to make changes, and so on. The properties of IT solutions become apparent over time while an application is used productively, evolves to meet new requirements, has to cope with failures, or has to be updated to newer versions. During this life cycle of an application, designers can reflect on the IT solution to determine whether it was well designed to meet such challenges.

2. Patterns in CRM

   Traditional marketing theory and practice has always assumed that enhancing revenues and maximizing profits can be achieved by expanding the customer base. While this may be a viable strategy, it may not hold true at all times. For instance, in mature industries and mature markets, customer acquisition may not hold the key to better financial performance: higher acquisition rates and retention rates do not necessarily result in higher profitability. While key customer metrics such as acquisition, retention, churn, and win-back are essential for establishing a profitable CRM strategy, merely "maximizing" each of these individual metrics is not necessarily a guarantee for success. Implementing specific and tailored strategies for key customer metrics yields a greater impact on customer decisions and can therefore lead to higher profitability. Prevailing patterns in CRM data can help in developing these specific strategies in each of the four steps of the customer–firm relationship life cycle: acquisition, retention, churn, and win-back.

a. *Acquisition*: The acquisition strategy involves attaining the highest possible customer acquisition rate by implementing mass-level strategies. Any combination of mass marketing (radio, billboards, etc.) and direct marketing (telemarketing, mail, email, etc.) could be implemented in order to target "eligible" customers rather than "interested" ones. A new approach to CRM pertaining to customer acquisition is gaining ground: there is a conscious move from mass marketing of products to one that is focused on the end consumer. Differentiating and segmenting with regard to demographic, psychographic, or purchasing power–related characteristics became more affordable and possible, and eventually became necessary in order to keep up with competing firms. As firms have become more capable and committed to data analyses, offerings have become more specific, thus increasing the amount of choice for customers. This has in turn spurred customers to expect more choice and customization in their purchases. It is through the continued improvements and innovations in data collection, storage, and analysis that acquisition has moved toward one-to-one acquisition.

b. *Retention*: Since the early 1960s, companies have changed their focus from short-term acquisition and transactions to long-term relationships and Customer Lifetime Value (CLTV). In fact, retention studies indicate that for every 1% improvement in customer retention rate, a firm's value increases by 5%.

c. *Churn or attrition*: Many firms fail to realize is that the majority of customers who are in the churn stage will not complain or voice their concerns. A study on this found that an estimated 4% of customers in the churn stage will actually voice their opinions, with the other 96% lost without voicing their discontent. Further, about 91% of the lost customers will never be won back.

d. *Win back*: Although re-acquiring lost customers may be a hard sell, it has been found that firms still have a 20–40%

chance of selling to lost customers versus only a 5–20% chance of selling to new prospects.

9.2 Domain-Specific Decision Patterns

In the following, we discuss as illustrations, decision patterns for two domains or functional areas, namely finance and customer relationship management (CRM). While the former is a formalized area to a large degree because of the statutory and regulatory requirements, the latter is defined and fine-tuned, across an extended period of operational experience, by the specific requirements of the business, offerings, and geographic region(s) in which the company operates.

9.2.1 Financial Decision Patterns

Financial management focuses on both the acquisition of financial resources on as favorable terms as possible and the utilization of the assets that those financial resources have been used to purchase, as well as looking at the interaction between these two activities. Financial planning and control is an essential part of the overall financial management process. Establishment of precisely what the financial constraints are and how the proposed operating plans will impact them are a central part of the finance function. This is generally undertaken by the development of suitable aggregate decision patterns like financial plans that outline the financial outcomes that are necessary for the organization to meet its commitments. Financial control can then be seen as the process by which such plans are monitored and necessary corrective action proposed when significant deviations are detected.

Financial plans are constituted of three decision patterns:

1. *Cash flow planning*: This is required to ensure that cash is available to meet the payments the organization is obliged to meet. Failure to manage cash flows will result in technical insolvency (the inability to meet payments when they are legally required to be made). Ratios are a set of powerful tools to report these matters. For focusing on cash flows and liquidity, a range of ratios based on working capital are appropriate;

each of these ratios addresses a different aspect of the cash collection and payment cycle.

The five key ratios that are commonly calculated are:

- Current ratio, equal to current assets divided by current liabilities
- Quick ratio (or acid test), equal to quick assets (current assets less inventories) divided by current liabilities
- Inventory turnover period, equal to inventories divided by the cost of sales, with the result being expressed in terms of days or months
- Debtors to sales ratio, with the result again being expressed as an average collection period
- Creditors to purchases ratio, again expressed as the average payment period.

There are conventional values for each of these ratios (e.g., the current ratio often has a standard value of 2.0 mentioned, although this has fallen substantially in recent years because of improvements in the techniques of working capital management, and the quick ratio a value of 1.0), but in fact these values vary widely across firms and industries. More generally helpful is a comparison with industry norms and an examination of the changes in the values of these ratios over time that will assist in the assessment of whether any financial difficulties may be arising.

2. *Profitability*: This is the need to acquire resources (usually from revenues acquired by selling goods and services) at a greater rate than using them (usually represented by the costs of making payments to suppliers, employees, and others). Although, over the life of an enterprise, total net cash flow and total profit are essentially equal, in the short term they can be very different. In fact, one of the major causes of failure for new small business enterprises is not that they are unprofitable but that the growth of profitable activity has outstripped the cash necessary to resource it. The major difference between profit and cash flow is in the acquisition of capital assets (i.e., equipment that is bought and paid for immediately, but that has likely benefits stretching over a considerable future period) and

timing differences between payments and receipts (requiring the provision of working capital).

For focusing on long-term profitability with short-term cash flows, profit to sales ratios can be calculated (although different ratios can be calculated depending whether profit is measured before or after interest payments and taxation). Value added (sales revenues less the cost of bought-in supplies) ratios can also be used to give insight into operational efficiencies.

3. *Assets*: Assets entail the acquisition and, therefore, the provision of finance for their purchase. In accounting terms, the focus of attention is on the balance sheet, rather than the profit and loss (P/L) account or the cash flow statement.

For focusing on the raising of capital as well as its uses, a further set of ratios based on financial structure can be employed. For example, the ratio of debt to equity capital (gearing or leverage) is an indication of the risk associated with a company's equity earnings (because debt interest is deducted from profit before obtaining profit distributable to shareholders). It is often stated that fixed assets should be funded from capital raised on a long-term basis, while working capital should fund only short-term needs.

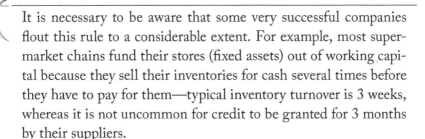

It is necessary to be aware that some very successful companies flout this rule to a considerable extent. For example, most supermarket chains fund their stores (fixed assets) out of working capital because they sell their inventories for cash several times before they have to pay for them—typical inventory turnover is 3 weeks, whereas it is not uncommon for credit to be granted for 3 months by their suppliers.

There is, therefore, no definitive set of financial ratios that can be said to measure the performance of a business entity. Rather, a set of measures can be devised to assess different aspects of financial performance from different perspectives. Although some of these measures can be calculated externally, being derived from annual financial reports, and can be used to assess the same aspect of financial performance across different companies, care needs to be taken to ensure that the same accounting principles have been used to produce the accounting numbers in each case. It is not uncommon for creative accounting to occur so that acceptable results can be reported. This draws attention especially to the interface between management accounting (which is intended to be useful in internal decision-making and control) and financial accounting (which is a major mechanism by which external stakeholders, especially shareholders, may hold managers accountable for their oversight).

Financial scandals, such as those at Enron and WorldCom, have highlighted that a considerable amount of such manipulation is possible within generally acceptable accounting principles (GAAPs). There is clear evidence that financial numbers alone are insufficient to reveal the overall financial condition of an enterprise. Part of the cause has been the rules-based approach of USA financial reporting, in contrast to the principle-based approach adopted in the United Kingdom. One result of the reforms that have followed these scandals has been a greater emphasis on operating information. In addition, legislation such as the Sarbanes–Oxley Act (SOX) in the United States has required much greater disclosure of the potential risks surrounding an enterprise, reflected internally by much greater emphasis on risk management and the maintenance of risk registers.

The finance function serves a boundary role; it is an intermediary between the internal operations of an enterprise and the key external stakeholders who provide the necessary financial resources to keep the organization viable. Decision patterns like financial ratios allow internal financial managers to keep track of a company's financial performance (perhaps in comparison with that of its major competitors) and to adjust the activities of the company, both operating and financial, so as to stay within acceptable bounds. A virtuous circle can be constructed whereby net cash inflows are sufficient to pay adequate returns to financiers and also contribute toward new investment; given sound profitability, the financiers will usually be willing to make additional investment to finance growth and expansion beyond that possible with purely internal finance. Conversely, a vicious cycle can develop when inadequate cash flows preclude adequate new invest-ment, causing a decline in profitability, and so the company becomes unable to sustain itself.

9.2.2 CRM Decision Patterns

This section gives an overview of the statistical models-based decision patterns used in CRM applications as the guiding concept for profit-able customer management. The primary objectives of these systems are to acquire profitable customers, retain profitable customers, pre-vent profitable customers from migrating to competition, and winning back "lost" profitable customers. These four objectives collectively lead to increasing the profitability of an enterprise.

CRM strategies spanning the full customer life cycle consist of four decision patterns or models:

1. *Customer acquisition*: The objectives of customer acquisition modeling includes identifying the right customers to acquire, predicting whether customers will respond to company pro-motion campaigns, forecasting the number of new customers, and examining the short- and long-term effects of marketing and other business variables on customer acquisition.

   This is a conscious move from mass marketing of prod-ucts to one that is focused on the end consumer. This is a direct result of increases in data collection and storage capa-bilities that have uncovered layer upon layer of customer dif-ferentiation. Differentiating and segmenting with regard to demographic, psychographic, or purchasing power–related characteristics became more affordable and possible, and eventually became necessary in order to keep up with com-peting firms. Although segment-level acquisition did not take this theory to the extent that one-to-one customer acquisi-tion has, it reinforced a growing trend of subsets or groups of customers within a larger target market. Being able to collect, store, and analyze customer data in more practical, affordable, and detailed ways has made all of this possible. As firms have become more capable and committed with data analyses, offerings have become more specific, thus increasing the amount of choice for customers. This has in turn spurred customers to expect more choice and customization in their purchases. This continuous firm–customer interaction has consistently shaped segment-level marketing practices in the process to better understand customers.

The decision patterns would incorporate:

- Differences between customers acquired through promotions and those acquired through regular means
- Effect of marketing activities and shipping and transportation costs on acquisition
- Impact of the depth of price promotions
- Differences in the impact of marketing-induced and word-of-mouth customers
- Return on customer equity

2. *Customer retention*: This involves decisions on who will buy, what the customers will buy, when they will buy, how much they will buy, and so on. During the customer's interaction with the firm, the firm may be interested in retaining this customer for a longer period of time. This calls for investigation of the role of trust and commitment to the firm, metrics for customer satisfaction, and the role of loyalty and reward programs, among others. The objective of customer retention modeling includes examining the factors influencing customer retention, predicting customers' propensity to stay with the company or terminate the relationship, and predicting the duration of the customer–company relationship. Customer retention strategies are used in both contractual (where customers are bound by contracts such as cell (mobile) phone subscription or magazine subscription) and noncontractual settings (where customers are not bound by contracts such as grocery purchases or apparel purchases).

Who to retain can often be a difficult question to answer. This is because the cost of retaining some customers can exceed their future profitability and thus make them unprofitable customers. When to engage in the process of customer retention is also an important component. As a result, firms must monitor their acquired customers appropriately to ensure that their customer loyalty is sustained for a long period of time. Finally, identifying how much to spend on a customer is arguably the most important piece of the customer retention puzzle. It is very easy for firms to over-communicate with a customer and spend more on his/her retention than the customer will ultimately give back to the firm in value.

The decision patterns would incorporate:
- Explaining customer retention or defection
- Predicting the continued use of the service relationship through the customer's expected future use and overall satisfaction with the service
- Renewal of contracts using dynamic modeling
- Modeling the probability of a member lapsing at a specific time using survival analysis
- Use of loyalty and reward programs for retention
- Assessing the impact of a reward program and other elements of the marketing mix

3. *Customer attrition or churn*: This involves decisions on whether the customer will churn or not, and if so what will be the probability of the customer churning and when. The objective of customer attrition modeling includes churn with time-varying covariates, mediation effects of customer status and partial defection on customer churn, churn using two cost-sensitive classifiers, dynamic churn using time-varying covariates, factors inducing service switching, antecedents of switching behavior, and impact of price reductions on switching behavior.

Engaging in active monitoring of acquired and retained customers is the most crucial step in being able to determine which customers are likely to churn. Determining who is likely to churn is an essential step. This is possible by monitoring customer purchase behavior, attitudinal response, and other metrics that help identify customers who feel under-appreciated or under-served. Customers who are likely to churn do demonstrate "symptoms" of their dissatisfaction, such as fewer purchases, lower response to marketing communications, longer time between purchases, and so on.

The collection of customer data is therefore crucial in being able to identify and capture such "symptoms," and that would help in analyzing the retention behavior and the choice of communication medium. Understanding who to save among those customers who are identified as being in the churn phase is again a question of cost versus future profitability.

The decision patterns would incorporate:

- When are the customers likely to defect?
- Can we predict the time of churn for each customer?
- When should we intervene and save the customers from churning?
- How much do we spend on churn prevention with respect to a particular customer?

4. *Customer win-back*: This involves decisions on re-acquiring the customer after the customer has terminated the relationship with the firm. The objective of customer win-back modeling includes customer lifetime value, optimal pricing strategies for recapture of lost customers, and the perceived value of a win-back offer.

Identifying the right customers to win back depends on factors such as the interests of the customers to reconsider their choice of quitting, the product categories that would interest the customers, the stage of customer life cycle, and so on. If understanding what to offer customers in winning them back is an important step in the win-back process, measuring the cost of win-back is as important as determining who to win back and what to offer them. The cost of win-back, much like the cost of retention or churn, must be juxtaposed with the customer's future profitability and value to the firm.

9.2.2.1 CRM Decision Patterns through Data Mining CRM systems like SAP CRM are used to track and efficiently organize inbound and outbound interactions with customers, including the management of marketing campaigns and call centers. These systems, referred to as operational CRM systems, typically support frontline processes in sales, marketing and customer service, and automating communications and interactions with the customers. They record contact history and store valuable customer information. They also ensure that a consistent picture of the customer's relationship with the organization is available at all customer "touch" (interaction) points. These systems are just tools that should be used to support the strategy of effectively managing customers.

However, to succeed with CRM, organizations need to gain insight into customers, their needs and wants through data analysis. This is where analytical CRM comes in. Analytical CRM is about analyzing customer information to better address the CRM objectives and deliver the right message to the right customer. It involves the use of data mining models in order to assess the value of the customers and understand and predict their behavior. It is about analyzing data patterns to extract knowledge for optimizing the customer relationships. For example,

- Data mining can help in customer retention as it enables the timely identification of valuable customers with increased likelihood to leave, allowing time for targeted retention campaigns.
- Data mining can support customer development by matching products with customers and better targeting of product promotion campaigns.
- Data mining can also help to reveal distinct customer segments, facilitating the development of customized new products and product offerings which better address the specific preferences and priorities of the customers.

The results of the analytical CRM procedures should be loaded and integrated into the operational CRM frontline systems so that all customer interactions can be more effectively handled on a more informed and "personalized" basis.

Marketers strive to get a greater market share and a greater share of their customers, that is, they are responsible for getting, developing, and keeping the customers. Data mining aims to extract knowledge and insight through the analysis of large amounts of data using sophisticated modeling techniques; it converts data into knowledge and actionable information. Data mining models consist of a set of rules, equations, or complex functions that can be used to identify useful data patterns and understand and predict behaviors.

Data mining models are of two kinds:

1. *Predictive or Supervised Models*: In these models, there are input fields or attributes and an output or target field. Input fields are also called predictors because they are used by the model to identify a prediction function for the output or target field. The model generates an "input–output" mapping function which associates predictors with the output so that, given the values of input fields, it predicts the output values. Predictive models themselves are of two types, namely classification or propensity models and estimation models. Classification models are predictive models with a predefined target field or classes or groups, so that the objective is to predict a specific occurrence or event. The model also assigns a propensity score with each of these events that indicates the likelihood of the occurrence of that event. In contrast, estimation models are used to predict a continuum of target values based on the corresponding input values.

2. *Undirected or Unsupervised Models*: In these models, there are input fields or attributes, but no output or target field. The goal of such models is to uncover data patterns in the set of input fields. Undirected models are also of two types, namely cluster models, and association and sequence models. Cluster models do not have a predefined target field or classes or groups, but the algorithms analyze the input data patterns and identify the natural groupings of cases. In contrast, association or sequence models do not involve or deal with the prediction of a single field. Association models detect associations between discrete events, products, or attributes; sequence models detect associations over time.

Data mining can provide customer insight, which is vital for establishing an effective CRM strategy. It can lead to personalized interactions with customers and hence increased satisfaction and profitable customer relationships through data analysis. It can support an "individualized" and optimized customer management throughout all the phases of the customer life cycle, from the acquisition and establishment of a strong relationship to the prevention of attrition and the winning back of lost customers.

1. *Segmentation*: This is the process of dividing the customer base into distinct and internally homogeneous groups in order to develop differentiated marketing strategies according to their characteristics. There are many different segmentation types based on the specific criteria or attributes used for segmentation. In behavioral segmentation, customers are grouped by behavioral and usage characteristics. Data mining can uncover groups with distinct profiles and characteristics and lead to rich segmentation schemes with business meaning and value. Clustering algorithms can analyze behavioral data, identify the natural groupings of customers, and suggest a solution founded on observed data patterns.

   Data mining can also be used for the development of segmentation schemes based on the current or expected/estimated value of the customers. These segments are necessary in order to prioritize customer handling and marketing interventions according to the importance of each customer.

2. *Direct Marketing Campaigns*: Marketers use direct marketing campaigns to communicate a message to their customers through mail, the internet, email, telemarketing (phone), and other direct channels in order to prevent churn (attrition) and to drive customer acquisition and purchase of add-on products. More specifically, acquisition campaigns aim at drawing new and potentially valuable customers away from the competition. Cross-/deep-/up-selling campaigns are implemented to sell additional products, more of the same product, or alternative but more profitable products to existing customers. Finally, retention campaigns aim at preventing valuable customers from terminating their relationship with the organization.

   Although potentially effective, this can also lead to a huge waste of resources and to bombarding and annoying customers with unsolicited communications. Data mining and classification (propensity) models in particular can support the development of targeted marketing campaigns. They analyze customer characteristics and recognize the profiles or extended profiles of the target customers.

3. *Market Basket Analysis*: Data mining and association models in particular can be used to identify related products typically purchased together. These models can be used for market basket analysis and for revealing bundles of products or services that can be sold together.

9.3 Summary

Architectural patterns capture the essential properties required for the successful design of a certain building area or function while leaving large degrees of freedom to architects. This chapter introduces the concept of the patterns and illustrates it by a discussion of decision patterns in finance and customer relationship management. This concept is then employed for defining performance decision patterns in the next chapter.

10

PERFORMANCE
DECISION PATTERNS

This chapter introduces the concept of performance, performance patterns, and their measurement. It discusses both cost and non-cost performance drivers. It not only refers to costs, but also to productivity performance, the level of inventories, and the saturation of productive capacity. The chapter discusses cost performance measurement and relationships between costs, productivity, and efficiency. The later part of the chapter assesses "noncost" performances, their dimensions and indicators. The presentation and approach in this chapter adopted from S. Tonchia and L. Quagini (2010).

10.1 Performance

A performance measure is the value assumed by an indicator of performance. The performance will be ex ante an *objective* of performance and ex post a *result* of performance. Only those managerial variables that can be influenced by the decision-making/action process are eligible to be considered as performance indicators, especially at the beginning during the planning phase while setting the goals and objectives, and at the end during the control phase while evaluating the outcomes or results. Key performance indicators (KPI) are algorithms that process a series of information relating to a process, or a part thereof, producing a result which is a parameter that denotes the trend or a significant component of the causes which determine the same.

The core business or management can be considered to involve the analysis and subsequent decisions regarding the relationship between operational performance and drivers. Consequently, performance measurement is a fundamental part of business management, as it allows the organization to understand:

- Where the organization was earlier
- Where the organization is today
- Where the organization wants to go
- How the organization will know when it gets there

In the past, accounting or cost performance systems were the only type of performance measurement systems available. Current performance measurement systems tend, however, to consist of, on the one hand, reviewed and updated accounting systems and, on the other, a system evaluating customer satisfaction and noncost performances (quality, time, and flexibility).

10.2 Cost Performance Drivers

10.2.1 Company Performance

The annual report is the main accounting document produced by companies. In addition to being a statutory tax obligation, it also provides an important overview of the economic and financial performance of the company. In particular, it not only highlights turnover, breakdown of costs, and therefore profits for the year, but it also allows readers to calculate a number of indices starting with the company's rate of profitability.

By comparing various aggregates of balance sheet entries and items, it is possible to construct the balance sheet indicators, the most important being:

1. Return On Equity (ROE), the ratio between profit and equity
2. Return On Assets (ROA), the ratio of operating income (Earnings Before Taxes, EBT), and total assets
3. Return On Investments (ROI), the ratio of operating income on core business operations (Earnings Before Interests and Taxes, EBIT) and assets net of financial entries
4. Return On Sales (ROS), the ratio of operating income on core business operations (EBIT) and sales revenue
5. Rotation of invested capital, the ratio between revenue and assets minus the financial entries

6. Rotation of receivables, the ratio between revenues and trade accounts receivable (the inverse determines the collection time of receivables)
7. Rotation of payables, the ratio between purchases and trade accounts payable (the inverse determines the accounts payable time; the difference, which is hopefully positive, between the payments time of accounts payable and the collection time of accounts receivable determines the so-called Cash Conversion cycle)
8. Liquidity, the ratio between immediate and delayed liquidity (the latter essentially referring to accounts receivable) and current liabilities (a good value for this indicator is equal to 1)
9. Cash on hand, the ratio of current assets (given by cash in hand and deferred cash plus inventories) and current liabilities (a good value for this indicator is equal to 2).

ROE, which mainly interests shareholders, can be broken down into three different elements: a product of ROA, the debt ratio (the ratio between total assets and equity) and impact (return on operating income including financial management).

ROI is used to evaluate operating managers and can be broken down into two elements: ROS and the rotation rate of invested capital.

Turnover, EBIT, ROE, and ROI are the primary indicators of a company's performance and consequently, over time, the value of the company itself (in addition to shareholders' equity).

Another version of the debt ratio is given by the ratio between liabilities (or borrowed capital) and equity. This ratio is considered in the financial leverage equation, which links ROE to ROI:

$$ROE = ROI + \left[ROI + \frac{NI}{L} \right] \times \frac{L}{E} = ROI + \left[ROI + \frac{FI - FC - T}{L} \right] \times \frac{L}{E}$$

where NI is the net income, E the equity, A the assets, and L the liabilities; FI, FC, and T refer to financial income, financial costs, and taxes, respectively.

The terms inside the square brackets refer to financial leverages, the difference between interest receivable (operating profitability) and interest payable (basically interest on borrowed capital).

It is clear that satisfactory operating results (represented by ROI) may not necessarily correspond to a similar positive return on equity (ROE) due to a negative leverage effect (excessive financial costs).

10.2.2 Cost Performance

Costs are classified using a variety of methods:

- Nature or kind
- Variability of volumes
- Allocation to cost center or product
- Time

The difficulties encountered when attempting to conduct an accurate and reliable calculation of the full cost of a product consist of the allocation of indirect costs which, by definition, are not easy to allocate immediately to a specific product.

As the variable costs are normally fairly simple to allocate to a specific product (such as materials, direct labor, and energy expenses, the latter in relation to specific machines or single product lines and specific cycles in the case of multiproduct lines), variable costs and direct costs are used interchangeably.

Activity-Based Costing (ABC) is one of the most important innovative techniques used in cost accounting and was developed to meet the need to provide full costing of a product based on the allocation of indirect costs using a single or multiple criteria (direct labor, cost of materials, total machine hours per product).

ABC is a technique that aims to calculate the full cost of a product, starting from the cost of consumed resources. The allocation of resource costs to individual products is not performed via the cost centers, as is traditional common practice, but is mediated via the activities, that is, the activities consume resources but products consume activities and not resources.

The cost performances include:

1. The costs of resources used in the production processes or to provide services. The profit is the difference between revenue and costs.
2. The level of working capital, making particular reference to the physical aspects, that is, inventory. The impact on final performance is the cost of tied-up capital which is equal to the value of inventory multiplied by the average periodic costs of financial capital (interest payable).
3. The saturation level of plant, machinery, and equipment, that is, all resources subject to amortization. A 100% non-use of an amortizable resource is classified as a waste of resources, that is, an additional cost equal to the unused percentage.
4. The employee absenteeism rate.
5. The productivity of resources, human and otherwise.

Profitability indicator Return on Investment (ROI)

$$
\begin{aligned}
\mathrm{ROI} &= \left(\frac{\text{Profit}}{\text{Total Investment}} \right) \\
&= \left(\frac{\text{Total Revenue} - \text{Total Cost}}{\text{Output}} \right) \times \left(\frac{\text{Output}}{\text{Capacity}} \right) \\
&\quad \times \left(\frac{\text{Capacity}}{\text{Technical Investments}} \right) \times \left(\frac{\text{Technical Investments}}{\text{Total Investment}} \right) \\
&= \left(\frac{\dfrac{\text{Total Revenue}}{\text{Output}} - \text{Total Cost}}{\text{Output}} \right) \times \left(\frac{\text{Output}}{\text{Capacity}} \right) \\
&\quad \times \left(\frac{\text{Capacity}}{\text{Technical Investments}} \right) \times \left(\frac{\text{Technical Investments}}{\text{Total Investment}} \right)
\end{aligned}
$$

$$\text{Unit cost of Product} = \frac{\left(\text{Salary Costs} + \text{Cost of Materials} + \text{Fixed Costs}\right)}{\text{Output}}$$

$$= \frac{\text{Salary Costs}}{\text{Output}} + \frac{\text{Cost of Materials}}{\text{Output}} + \frac{\text{Fixed Costs}}{\text{Output}}$$

$$= \text{Hour Cost} \times \left(\frac{\text{Manhours}}{\text{Output}}\right) + \text{Material Unit Cost}$$

$$\times \left(\frac{\text{Material Units}}{\text{Output}}\right) + \left(\frac{\text{Capacity}}{\text{Output}}\right)$$

$$\times \left(\frac{\text{Fixed Costs}}{\text{Total Investments}}\right) \times \left(\frac{\text{Total Investments}}{\text{Capacity}}\right)$$

$$= \frac{\text{Hour Cost}}{\left(\dfrac{\text{Output}}{\text{Man Hours}}\right)} + \frac{\text{Material Unit Cost}}{\left(\dfrac{\text{Output}}{\text{Material Units}}\right)}$$

$$+ \frac{\left(\dfrac{\text{Fixed Costs}}{\text{Total Investments}}\right)}{\left(\dfrac{\text{Output}}{\text{Capacity}}\right) \times \left(\dfrac{\text{Capacity}}{\text{Total Investments}}\right)}$$

$$= \frac{\text{Hour Cost}}{\text{Labour Productivity}} + \frac{\text{Material Unit Cost}}{\text{Material Productivity}}$$

$$+ \frac{\text{Depreciation Rate}}{\text{Capital Expenditure Productivity}}$$

10.2.3 Productivity Performance

Productivity is the ratio between output and input, while efficiency is the ratio between productivity and a standard:

$$\text{Productivity} = \frac{\text{Actual Output}}{\text{Actual Input}}$$

$$\text{Efficiency} = \frac{\left(\dfrac{\text{Actual Output}}{\text{Standard Output}}\right)}{\left(\dfrac{\text{Actual Input}}{\text{Standard Input}}\right)}$$

Productivity is therefore expressed by a ratio between the quantity (or value) of a realized product and the quantity (or value) of used resources, while efficiency is expressed by a number, usually less than one unit (if the set goals or standards are aggresive).

Efficiency should not be confused with efficacy; efficacy is the ratio between actual output (or performance) and the desired output (or performance). Therefore, efficacy measures the ability to achieve goals, regardless of the input (resources) used.

The inverse productivity of a resource is represented by the standard cost for a resource; the latter is in fact the optimal cost in relation to one unit of output (given by the ratio: input value/output quantity, which is the exact inverse of productivity).

Productivity can be measured as:

- Organizational performance as a whole (total productivity)
- Performance in relation to the use of a specific resource (partial or "single-factor productivity")
- Performance obtained as a synthesis of partial results (weighted productivity, weighted sum of partial productivity).

    Types of partial productivity (defined by the Output/Input I_i ratio, ratio), include:
    - Labor productivity (direct and/or indirect)
    - Material productivity (which considers the quantified amounts of raw materials and components used to obtain the finished products)
    - Energy productivity (which compares machinery consumptions with the amount of production obtained)

The productivity of a combination of resources can be considered as:

$$\frac{O}{\Sigma_i I_i}$$

- Value-added productivity (where value added, defined as the difference between output value and input value, is compared to value of input after deducting the cost of materials).

  Productivity must not be achieved at the expense of quality, and therefore the output used in the productivity rate must refer to good products.

  Overall,

  Equipment Effectiveness (OEE) = Machine Availability × Efficiency × Quality Yield

  where Machine Availability is available time/total time and Quality Yield is good pieces/total pieces.

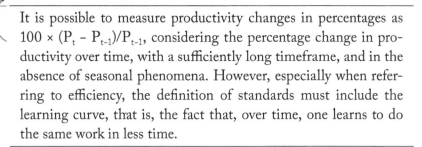

It is possible to measure productivity changes in percentages as $100 \times (P_t - P_{t-1})/P_{t-1}$, considering the percentage change in productivity over time, with a sufficiently long timeframe, and in the absence of seasonal phenomena. However, especially when referring to efficiency, the definition of standards must include the learning curve, that is, the fact that, over time, one learns to do the same work in less time.

10.3 Noncost Performance Drivers

10.3.1 Quality Performance

Quality is a multidimensional concept and therefore its measurement can only be achieved by dividing quality into several dimensions:

1. Quality costs, divided into:
   - Prevention/maintenance costs
   - Quality control/testing costs
   - Nonquality costs (or "negative quality")

2. Quality offered by the company, which can be broken down into:
   - In-bound quality (quality of supplies)
   - Internal, hence inside the company which, in turn, can be broken down into:
     - Product design
     - Engineering of the production process (process capability)
     - Production (conformance)
   - Out-bound quality (quality of distribution/delivery services)
3. Perceived quality and customer satisfaction, both in terms of products and services.

One can see that there is a crucial need to ensure that all the quality produced is also the quality perceived.

Quality performance is often not evaluated at an overall, integrated, and standardized level, and is limited mostly to single, and often repeated, onsite testing and control of product nonconformance. The measurement of quality is of fundamental importance: no quality improvement program, no quality-based competitive strategy can be implemented in the absence of a serious, practical, and comprehensive measurement of all the various aspects of quality.

Dimensions of quality are shown in Figure 10.1.

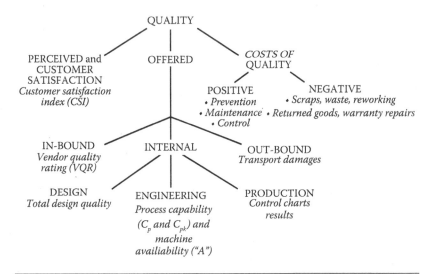

Figure 10.1   Dimensions of quality.

10.3.1.1 Engineering and Manufacturing Internal Quality Process quality performance or process capability (indicated as Cp) represents the probability that the produced units satisfy design specifications. In statistical terms, assuming that the law of large numbers is applied (high-volume production), it can be said that the various measures of conformity distribute their values according to a Gaussian form of distribution, also called normal or bell-shaped. From a design point of view, every measurement has a target value and a tolerance range in relation to such a target, within which the product may still be considered compliant. From a production standpoint, the realizations for each parameter being measured refer to an average value of m and a standard deviation of s, values which hence create the Gaussian curve. Since the entire area below the curve is 1, by its own definition, the area enclosed by the curve and the design specifications represent the fraction of conforming products (for the x-parameter being considered).

Production quality performance is recognized as a result of specific monitoring of produced unit conformity. Simple tools can be used such as histograms, pareto charts, fishbone diagrams, and also more sophisticated control charts. Control charts allow you to monitor several key product variables (or process variables that have an impact on product variables), highlighting any deviations where the values exceed the "control range" defined in each chart; this area is created by a bottom threshold and an upper threshold, both created on a statistical basis: the purpose of the control charts is not, in fact, to emphasize the actual level of quality, but to highlight any deviations from the usual results. The charts can control discrete values (e.g., conforming/nonconforming) or continuous values (a measure of the product or production process).

10.3.1.2 Purchasing and Vendor Quality Rating Incoming quality is correlated with the performance of suppliers and the efficacy of the purchasing department in pursuing company objectives (selection, evaluation, and management of approved suppliers). After choosing certain suppliers, incoming quality is expressed as

- The quality of supplies (i.e., objects)
- Supply process quality (i.e., transactions)

On the one hand, we have a quality performance in the strictest sense of the term (conformance with specifications) and on the other the quality performance relating to supply-related activities (meeting deadlines, quantities, and agreed mix—in this case, performance is justly related to the temporal dimension, estimations upstream of external time performance or downstream in relation to the company).

The purchasing department, using complete control procedures or sample statistical techniques, must ensure conformity of:

- The delivered units (whose defects can be reported in a Pareto analysis in terms of amounts and severity)
- The integrity of deliveries (with bar graphs showing the delays/early deliveries of complete orders).

Vendor Quality Rating (VQR) is one of the main tools used when evaluating suppliers, in addition to traditional considerations of price and timeliness/punctuality of deliveries.

The VQR is generally understood as the ratio of accepted lots (L_{acc}) and the sum of accepted lots and rejected lots for various reasons "i" (L_{ri}), the latter weighted (with factors p_i) according to the severity of the defects:

$$VQR = \frac{L_{acc}}{\left(L_{acc} + p_1 L_{r1} + p_2 L_{r2} + p_3 L_{r3}\right)}$$

It is important to note that the weights p_i relate to fair evaluation of the economic damage generated by a nonconformity, and not to individual types of nonconformity (which can number in the hundreds).

10.3.1.3 Quality Costs   Quality is not "free of charge" as some of the slogans used in the past tended to claim, but is an investment made to achieve greater customer satisfaction and, hence, turnover and/or a decrease in internal costs.

Quality costs include:

1. Prevention/maintenance (including costs for management procedures and quality programs, for the selection/evaluation of suppliers, and for preventive maintenance)
2. Cost of quality control/final testing and inspection (both in terms of human and instrumental resources)

3. Nonquality costs including: internally speaking, the costs incurred for the scrapping of finished products, the scrapping of processed materials, and reworking costs; and externally speaking, the products returned by customers and/or the cost of warranty services (labor and parts).

10.3.2 Time Performance

A matrix can be used to illustrate the classification of time performances, based on dimensions of internal/external performance and their short/long-term features in relation to production/delivery cycles and product-development cycles (Table 10.1).

Where time performances use time as the unit of measure (such as lead times, order handling times, and time-to-market), the time should be specified in terms of the average value and the standard deviation, or at least indicating—apart from the average value—the maximum and minimum values; moreover, it may be more important to measure the decrease in times—also percentage-wise—rather than the absolute magnitude of the times themselves. The other cases (conformance with schedules, machine availability, timeliness, and completeness of deliveries, and frequency of introduction/modification of products) refer to ratios and are therefore dimensionless.

Throughput time is defined:

- In industrial engineering, as the time between the completion of two different units of production (i.e., the time interval between two successive units in the input or output section, also referred to as the production rate)
- In material management, as the time period between the input and output of a specific unit of material in a manufacturing plant (also called lead time).

Table 10.1 Time Performance Classification

	INTERNAL PERFORMANCES	EXTERNAL PERFORMANCES
Short-term performances (Production/delivery)	• (Purchasing/production/ distribution) lead times • Adherence to scheduling	• Readiness • Punctuality • Delivery reliability
Long-term performances (Product development)	• Machine availability • Time-to-market	• Product innovation (frequent introduction)

Lead time can refer to all types of time periods that can be encountered in all manufacturing industries (i.e., customer order lead-times, design lead time, further to production, distribution, and supply lead times) or also a cumulative lead time.

Often production lead time is considered as the sum of four different phases (cycle time):

1. Run or process time
2. Wait or queue time
3. Set-up time
4. Move time

Adherence-to-schedule measures the degree of deviation between the actual and estimated dates of the start/end of each internal operation, and clearly influences the timeliness of delivery; it can be measured by the ratio: (scheduled orders—completed orders)/(scheduled orders), where scheduled orders refer to manufacturing orders which were to be completed in a given reference period, while completed orders refers to the manufacturing orders actually completed in that same period.

Machine Availability ("A") is given, for each machine, by the ratio between the time the machine is available for processing and the total time (the latter includes, in addition to the time when the machine is available for processing, also time spent on preventive and reactive maintenance, that is interventions made following a machine failure).

Machine availability is also measured by the ratio:

$$\frac{\text{MTBF}}{(\text{MTBF} + \text{MTTR})},$$

where MTBF is the Mean Time Between Failures and MTTR is the Mean Time To Repair machinery.

The MTBF of machines, which is probability-based, is the main indicator of Machine Reliability ("R"), while MTTR, again probability-based, is the main indicator of Machine Maintainability ("M").

Reliability is the probability that a system fulfills its function satisfactorily for a specific period of time and under certain operating conditions; it is measured using:

- the Reliability function "R" (probability that a system will not fail before a set time
$$T: R(T) = Prob(t \geq T))$$
- the mean time before the first failure (MTTF, Mean Time To Failure) or between successive failures (MTBF, Mean Time Between Failures).

Maintainability is the probability that a system failure can be repaired within a specific time interval ("down-time"), including inspection and repair times; it is measured using:

- the Maintainability function "M" (probability that the inspection/repair time will be less than

$$T: M(t) = Prob(t \leq T))$$

- the Mean Time To Repair (MTTR).

Clearly, machine availability, and therefore its reliability and maintainability, are correlated with the productivity of the machine itself, as the amount of output produced over time, in relation to the same input, actually decreases, that is, the machine depreciation expense (which must be accounted for); furthermore, the cost of input can even increase if you also take into account the maintenance costs.

The term "six big losses" has also been coined to refer to the efficiency losses resulting from:

1. Unexpected failures
2. Set-ups and adjustments
3. Idle operations and short down-times
4. Decreases in speed
5. Waste during processing
6. Waste during the start-up phase

The short-term time performances perceived externally refer to timeliness, punctuality, and completeness of deliveries. Timeliness can be measured as the average lapse of time required to deliver an order. Punctuality can be measured as the percentage of orders delivered in a given period of time compared to the estimated target date, or alternatively as the mean delay or percentage mean delay (in the latter case, the actual delay time is calculated for each order as a percentage compared to the foreseen delivery target date).

Completeness (or reliability of deliveries with respect to quantity and mix; when referring to a date, however, it is intended as punctuality) can be measured as the average of the percentage of order lines actually delivered in relation to the number of lines which should have been delivered (each order in fact consists of multiple order lines), in relation to delivery punctuality.

Finally, as far as medium to long-term performances are concerned, customers perceive time dimensions via the innovative level of products (which must not be confused with the quality of the product), the frequency by which new models are introduced (in addition to or replacing existing ones), or substantial modifications to existing models; while, from an internal point of view, the total duration of the project or time-to-market can be measured, intended as the time from the product concept phase until it reaches mass production.

10.3.3 Flexibility Performance

Flexibility is often considered from a time performance point of view; it should however be seen as the ability to change something, not only quickly but with low costs and without decreasing quality; flexibility would therefore be in the center of the classic performance triad of cost/time/quality. In analytical terms, one could write:

$$\frac{\partial^3 O}{(\partial c \, \partial q \, \partial t)}$$

However, given that, in order to really speak of flexibility, the changes in costs (increases) and quality (decreases) should be much lower than the relative changes in times, as flexibility is often compared to a time performance: that is, only the change in the time denominator is taken into account.

Given the importance of flexibility and its interest to managers, its measurement still requires further development, due to both the multi imensional aspects that characterize flexibility and the lack of indicators that can measure it directly.

10.4 Summary

This chapter introduced the concept of performance, and performance patterns and their measurement. It discussed both cost and noncost performance drivers. The chapter discussed cost performance measurement and relationships between costs, productivity, and efficiency. The later part of the chapter assessed "noncost" performances and their dimensions of quality, time, and flexibility.

11

PERFORMANCE INTELLIGENCE

The effect of continuous adjustments and enhancements to business operations can generate a steady stream of savings and new revenues that may sometimes seem insignificant from one day to the next, but as months go by, may become cumulatively substantial. The profits generated in this way can be thought of as the agility dividend. Real-time data sharing and close coordination between business processes (sales, procurement, accounting, etc.) can be employed to deliver continuous operating adjustments that result in steady cost savings over time (negative feedback) as well as the delivery of timely new products and services to identified customers that result in significant new revenue (positive feedback).

A company can design and implement instruments ranging from decision patterns to performance intelligence (PI) systems that can enable continuous correction of business unit behavior in order for companies to achieve enhanced levels of productivity and profitability.

11.1 Performance Intelligence

PI provides the information required to control business processes and to take effective business decisions.

1. PI provides information to control business activity.

   PI provides information to control business activity regardless of where the information is stored. PI is an important component of the overall management information system, which controls the proper operation of business processes and activities. In a classic organization transformation or operational processes are affected by external events and environment perturbations (market changes, substitute products, new legislation, etc.). Under these situations, operational processes usually require some kind of control, adaptation, and correction. Without this supervision, business processes may tend toward disorganization and chaos.

Business control is achieved, for example, by means of some performance indicators. These indicators are properly quantified to analyze and evaluate the achievement of organizational objectives. Therefore, business control is a mechanism to find out if something is going wrong, or if something can be improved in the organization. Business activities and processes generate and consume information during their execution. Part of this information (operational information) is consumed in the short term, but most of it is stored in some mostly transactional system (ERP, CRM, SCM, etc.) until it is used for tactical (mid-term) or strategic (long-term) decision-making processes.

Operational information must be aggregated and made available to the control system in a timely manner, regardless of the operational system from which it comes. Therefore, it will be possible to modify and optimize organization processes. The levels of aggregation and required standardization of heterogeneous data sources will be higher as more strategic and decisional processes are addressed. This decisional nature of the process justifies the next core dimension or characteristic of PI: decision-making support.

2. PI gives support to decision-making processes.

PI not only provides information to users, it also allows the users to manage, browse, and analyze information on organizational behavior. Therefore, it is useful to find causes of problems and to identify improvement opportunities. Analysis is fundamental for decision-making activities. Decisions are not made on the basis of a single source of information. Various information sources are weighed up and inter related in real-time. Information analysis is what enables the user to make better business decisions.

3. The information provided by PI is business language oriented.

It is not possible to make effective business decisions if we do not talk the same business language. Regardless of where the information is stored and how it may have been transformed or aggregated, the key point is to provide this information to business users in their own language. They should understand the causes and consequences of their decisions, they must be comfortable with their decision, and they should not require reinterpretation of information provided using the terms they are familiar with. In this sense, PI must be information orientated toward the language of business users. In this way, user work is easier and the decision-making required to improve processes and to gain competitiveness is speeded up.

11.2 PI Methodology

The characteristics of PI methodology are:

1. *Alignment with business needs*: A PI methodology must control the alignment of IT development with business needs to provide value. Development must be linked with business strategy and also with business change.
2. *Change oriented*: A PI methodology must be more orientated to facilitate and manage change than to the achievement of a final product. Since the market, the provided services, and the business processes change constantly, the methodology must give effective support to manage this change in a dynamic way.
3. *Multi-project*: A PI methodology must be able to manage several (sub) projects at once and in parallel (ETL, cleansing data, reporting, queries, dashboards, scorecards, datamining, etc.).
4. *Focus on critical paths*: A PI methodology must use critical paths for management. This means that it must specially focus on critical tasks that would change the planning. Then, re-planning is only necessary when this path is affected.
5. *Cross-functional*: A PI methodology must be executed by a multidisciplinary team. Information does not belong to a single department, it is a resource for all the organization, and everyone must be involved in its provision and use. Processes of an organization are not isolated in only one department; they usually cross several department boundaries. Therefore, to control and manage the main processes of

the organization, it is necessary to follow a cross-functional and multidisciplinary approach.

6. *Comprehensive*: A PI methodology considers all tasks to be taken into account. Not having all tasks could result in a critical task being forgotten, and then it would be necessary to redo some work, with loss of efficiency and completeness.

7. *People focused*: In any organization some people make the decisions; other people actually perform, control, and decide on processes. All of them are focused on the management of structures and processes in a continuous way. We need effective mechanisms to foster relations between the people in the organization. We need to focus on people. We need to add a third additional component to "structures" and "processes." This component is the "relational mechanism." This mechanism will ensure the active participation and collaboration of key users from business and IT in interdisciplinary teams. These teams are those that will ensure value is provided to the organization and its use guaranteed.

11.2.1 PI Approaches

The most representative approaches used to deal with PI projects are described below.

1. Traditional Analysis Approach
   Basic Approach: In the traditional Software Development Lifecycle (SDLC) waterfall process, the basic approach involves translating user needs into software requirements by using an analysis step. Later, user requirements are transformed into a design architecture, which is implemented and tested. At the end, the software is delivered to users.
   Methodologies: Plan-Driven (like the Rational Unified Process) and Requirement-Driven methodologies.
   Strengths: This approach is the precursor of most existing methodologies since it is based on the origins of software engineering. This approach had been applied in many projects and under different situations; therefore such methodologies are well known since they have been tested and widely proven.

Weaknesses: There have been many attempts to apply methodologies based on requirements, but they have failed to
implement PI systems. The root of the problem is that
decision-making is always a semi-structured and rapidly
changing process, while these methodologies assume a
stable environment with minor changes and a definite
structure. This approach might not be able to appropriately handle frequent changes in the current and future
demands of users. Moreover, the difficulty for users to
describe and explain how they make their decisions may
be a problem for using this methodological approach.

2. User Driven Approach

Basic Approach: PI methodologies that follow this approach
are based on an early prototype construction based on
the business objectives. Given these objectives, users
will define their information needs, queries that will be
requested to the PI system, and the maintenance and
future development requirements. The importance of the
role and participation of the business users in the construction of PI systems is stated not only when the system is defined, but basically during all cognitive stages
of the decision-making process of the user (observation,
elemental abstraction, reasoning, symbolization, and creativity). Through these studies, we may infer that a PI system should be constructed based on the type of queries
the user will request (query adaptation) and the type of
responses that the system must provide (response adaptation). Therefore, as we have more knowledge of how users
"understand and process" the information, we are more
capable of designing a PI system.

Methodologies: Demand-Driven, User-Driven, and Prototype-
Driven methodologies.

Strengths: The most important advantage of this approach is its
complete orientation toward the system's use and the user
needs. The requirements are not completely defined to start
with, and thus these methodologies seek to show the user a
working prototype to try to capture the best possible business needs. These methodologies seek a well-defined user

interface, after trying to understand the user and the issues that he/she has to respond with respect to the business, especially the strategic questions. Many of the current projects that have been reported as successful by practitioners and software vendors are a combination of methodologies based on requirements management and on prototyping. Therefore, one success factor is precisely the user involvement and alignment with the real business needs.

Weaknesses: A weakness of this approach is to assume that all users know the business strategy and that they act consistently with it, when in fact this is not always the case. Therefore, generally those users who make decisions are those who must lead the PI system creation process.

3. Data-Driven Approach

Basic Approach: This approach is based on the hypothesis that "users lie, data don't." This approach is focused on the analysis of business data with a higher rate of access, data that are queried more frequently, and how different data are related. These "most useful" data guide the PI system design process.

Strengths: The strength of this approach is based on the appreciation that "data does not lie, let's use it." If a dataset is requested to build a PI system, it means that these data are needed. Following this approach, we can have a clear idea of what information is necessary for the user to achieve some functionality.

Weaknesses: Data-driven approaches leave the users and the business objectives out of consideration, but focus only on data usage. The problem is that this strategy could not properly identify the business, that is, the necessary control information, when this is not highly accessed. Additionally, this methodology may not be adequate to identify future business needs.

4. Process-Driven Approach

Basic Approach: This approach focuses on the analysis of how business processes are performed in the organization. A control process guides this approach, because if we have control over our own process we can provide value.

Strengths: The main strength of this methodology is its process orientation. Business processes must be controlled to ensure the daily operation and competitiveness of the organization. Therefore, processes must be monitored or linked by the PI system so they can be improved and controlled.

Weaknesses: In organizations, people manage processes and there are often dissonances between what processes define, the business needs, and what people decide. Isolating processes without taking into account cross-functional relationships may give us a false view of the organization operation. Moreover, if we only focus on processes, we cannot get a global overview. Besides, customers do not perceive the organization processes, they only perceive provided services, and thus a service orientation approach might be a better approach.

5. Event-Driven Approach

Basic Approach: The Event-Driven approach proposes to split business processes into three views: Data, Function and Organization, with all three connected to each other through events.

Strengths: The main strength is that it is an attempt to analyze the organization in a cross-functional way and also includes support functions to the processes.

Weaknesses: The weak point is that this approach is too complex to be implemented and requires much effort and high maturity models in the organization.

6. Goal-Driven Approach

Basic Approach: This approach focuses on the goals of the organization and its processes. It is based on analysis of the interaction between customers/providers and business users to achieve that goal. It is based on providing value to the customers to generate value to the organization, but it is not possible to generate value without the provider's participation. The PI system architecture is defined as the result of the analysis of information needs and relationships between them. Therefore, it is necessary to define the strategic goals and to direct the main effort to improving the relationships of customers and providers with the organization.

Strengths: The strength of this approach is that it is based on the company's strategic objectives and its real needs.

Weaknesses: This approach must consider the strategic objectives of the organization, but problems may appear if control processes do not consider explicitly the operational and tactical business objectives. The PI system provides support functions to control the organizational processes, but when the organization strategy is mistaken or tactical and operational objectives are unknown, this approach is not as successful as expected.

7. Model Driven Approach

Basic Approach: The Model Driven PI methodology seeks to bridge gaps between the business and the IT department. Its purpose is to provide the basis for developing quick solutions, which evolve easily and with high flexibility. The underlying idea is to develop a model to simplify business complexity and then to transform and deploy it in different system architectures, preferably in service-oriented architectures (SOA).

Strengths: Model Driven Development (MDD) has been widely applied in several areas, such as software reuse, re-engineering, and reverse design of user interfaces. Benefits of the MDD approach may include time reduction in software development, quality improvement, and quality maintenance. It is a simple evolution of prototyping that places more emphasis on semantic transformation.

Weaknesses: The approach is too technology dependent. It is not easy to simplify business complexity, and it is not easy to deploy SOA architectures in real business situations.

8. Adaptive Business Approach

Basic Approach: The Adaptive Business Approach is based uniquely on what is relevant to the business. It focuses on problems of the business to adapt to market changes and the data necessary to address this situation. The expected output of a PI system must either be a concrete solution to the problem or more knowledge about the problem to continue reasoning.

Strengths: The strongest point of this approach is that it focuses on change. Organizations are affected by marked changes and therefore they may become vulnerable, so focusing on change may allow more accurate decisions about the future to be made, permitting the organization to evolve.

Weaknesses: The weakness of this approach is that sometimes processes with lesser business value also need to be supported in order to execute the main (most value added) processes.

9. Agile Approach

Basic Approach: The Agile Manifesto defines four values that agile methodologies should follow:

- Individuals and interactions over processes and tools. Working software over comprehensive documentation. Customer collaboration over contract negotiation. Responding to change over following a plan.

Methodologies: Agile Modeling, Agile Unified Process (AUP), Dynamic Systems Development Method (DSDM), Essential Unified Process (EssUP), Extreme Programming (XP), Feature Driven Development (FDD), Open Unified Process (OpenUP), Scrum, etc.

Strengths: This approach can help us to search for a better PI methodology, contributing easily with five of the seven characteristics that a PI project must have:
- Alignment with business needs
- Change oriented
- Multi-project
- Cross-functional
- People focused

Weaknesses: Lacks industrial successful cases trackrecord.

11.3 Agile Principles

The Agile Manifesto also distinguishes 12 principles that characterize an agile process. Those 12 principles had not been sufficiently implemented in more traditional approaches.

Traditional approaches consider them in some way, but without enough emphasis. Agile approaches focus in more depth on these principles, trying to solve the main gaps in software development methodologies.

The 12 principles are listed in Table 11.1:

Table 11.1   12 Agile Principles

P1 (Continuous delivery of value)	Our highest priority is to satisfy the customer through early and continuous delivery of valuable software.
P2 (Welcome changes)	We welcome changing requirements, even late in development. Agile processes harness change for the customer's competitive advantage.
P3 (Frequent deliveries)	Deliver working software frequently, from a couple of weeks to a couple of months, with a preference for the shorter timescale.
P4 (Working together)	Business people and developers must work together daily throughout the project.
P5 (Motivated individuals)	Build projects around motivated individuals. Give them the environment and support they need, and trust them to get the job done.
P6 (Face-to-face conversation)	The most efficient and effective method of conveying information to and within a development team is face-to-face conversation.
P7 (Working software)	Working software is the primary measure of progress.
P8 (Sustainable development)	Agile processes promote sustainable development. The sponsors, developers, and users should be able to maintain a constant pace indefinitely.
P9 (Attention to excellence)	Continuous attention to technical excellence and good design enhances agility.
P10 (Simplicity)	Simplicity (the art of maximizing the amount of work not done) is essential.
P11 (Self-organizing teams)	The best architectures, requirements, and designs emerge from self-organizing teams.
P12 (Reflects and adjusts)	At regular intervals, the team reflects on how to become more effective, then tunes and adjusts its behavior accordingly.

11.4 PI Delivery Framework

The PI delivery framework involves six phases, namely, discovery, architecture, design, development, testing and deployment.

11.4.1 Discovery

Most of what can and cannot be delivered is determined by data quality and availability. Once data sources have been identified, the next step requires gaining an understanding of the data. Data profiling focuses on two phases:

1. Values analysis
2. Structure analysis

Data profiling provides data demographics and descriptive statistics such as frequency distribution, high and low values, blank attributes and records, exceptions to domain values, dependencies between attributes, unknown constraints, mean, median, mode, and standard deviation. The knowledge gained from analyzing data demographics provides the basis for data quality metrics and can be used later in the life cycle for modeling, development, and testing. Most importantly, assumptions about the data and information capabilities are removed. With this knowledge, information needs can be prioritized and increments planned.

The first phase is the discovery phase where stakeholders determine information requirements. Information requirements begin with defining business questions which provide insight into data sources, dimensions, and facts needed.

11.4.2 Architecture

At the beginning of a PI program, the architecture needs to be established. Creating a flexible, scalable architecture is essential to supporting growth.

PI architecture includes business, technical, process, data, and project architecture. PI business architecture centers on defining the drivers, goals, and strategy of the organization that drive information needs. Process architecture includes a framework for tackling data acquisition to data presentation. Data architecture addresses how data will be structured in data repositories, such as a data mart or warehouse. PI technology architecture includes hardware, PI software, and networks required to deliver PI projects. PI project architecture describes the incremental methodology used for short, small releases. If the PI architecture is established, design will center on modeling data and processes to support information needs. Models created in this phase could include conceptual, logical, and physical data models as well as process models for ETL.

Envisioning the architecture begins with diagramming. Diagrams work well in the Agile paradigm as they are easily altered and maintained versus text-based documents. Diagrams include data models, data flows, process flows, and infrastructure diagrams. With technical architecture, the deliverable can be a diagram outlining the different technologies required. The beginnings of the data architecture can be a conceptual subject-level model.

Diagrams are a beginning, but they do not test out the architectural vision. Architecture decisions once implemented cannot be easily reversed. The approach of a reference implementation works well in the Agile paradigm. Like a prototype, a reference implementation is a working model but focuses on testing out the architecture. Reference implementations for ETL architecture, for example, can demonstrate if service levels are possible and remove assumptions about the technology. A proof of concept (POC) is also another approach used in validating architectural decisions. POCs are often used in PI due to organizations using the best-of-breed approach. The best-of-breed approach is defined as organizations choosing independent tools, such as ETL and databases, which need to be integrated as part of the technical architecture. Although reference implementations and POCs are used in traditional software development, in PI they become the rule.

11.4.3 Design

The activities completed in the design phase of the PI framework are modeling and mapping. These activities are iterative in nature and use the output of the discovery phase. Data profiling analysis and high-level architectural diagrams provide the context for design.

Modeling in this framework is focused on prioritized requirements, data demographics, and a stable scope for the increment. Business questions provide an understanding of how data will be used and data demographics assist the modeler in identifying business transactions, uniqueness, and primary/foreign key relationships. The modeling iteration is shortened through the use of data discovery early in the project. The modeling iteration may include a completed logical or physical model; however, due to the iterative cycles, the models may be a first pass. At a minimum, models will demonstrate behavioral and informational semantics.

Models can represent sources and targets. Mapping the data between the source and target is an essential design activity. The source to target mapping will be evolutionary within the scope of the increment. The exercise of mapping confirms data understanding and discovers business, transformation, and cleansing rules.

By having models and source to target mappings, development on ETL and end-user capabilities can begin. Refinements to the design can occur via development iterations. Subject matter experts from the business and IT collaborate to clarify and refine design throughout the increment.

11.4.4 Development

PI development may include a wide array of activities. The primary focus of the development phase is to produce a working system that applies business context to data and presents information in a way that enables end users to analyze actionable information. Activities could include coding ETL, configuring logical layers in a PI tool, or scripting scheduling jobs. The scope of development can involve data acquisition to staging, staging to presentation, and presentation to the access and delivery of information.

In an Agile paradigm, the goal of development is to deliver working software regularly. In PI, development deliverables can include ETL processes, analysis, or reporting capabilities. Different approaches to ETL exist such as Enterprise Application Integration (EAI), Enterprise Information Integration (EII), and Extract, Load, and Transform (ELT) which are out of scope for this discussion. Regardless of ETL approach, PI development includes an ETL deliverable. Development iterations focus on the delivery of requirements; however, the requirements are not delivered in the first cycle. Throughout the requirements and design iterations, stakeholders are working with the data to confirm understanding and remove assumptions. Development will produce software that enriches the data. The development iteration refines requirements and design through stakeholder collaboration. Stakeholders can confirm information results through validation of business rules and verification of output to alternate sources. Through development iterations, the scope that can be delivered in the allotted timeframe becomes clear.

At the conclusion of the development phase, requirements and design are concluded for the increment and the development deliverables are ready to be tested.

11.4.5 Testing

In an Agile paradigm, testing occurs constantly through the interactions of stakeholders. Collaboration with stakeholders ensures results are verified during the life cycle to produce higher quality results. Since PI systems tend to be complex, a formal change control process is recommended. Additionally, a regression test suite for the PI system is essential. With the fuzzy nature of information, it is possible to impact prior working functionality and not see the impact until after deployment.

11.4.6 Deployment

PI systems tend to be complex for many reasons. One reason for complexity is that PI systems have many independent components that require integration. Another reason is PI systems are impacted by continuous change. Because of this complexity, the PI deployment phase is formal and controlled. Activities in this phase focus on integration of new functionality and capability into production, and regression testing to verify that previously working functionality is not impacted. Deployment focuses on the introduction of new components and maintaining the stability of the production PI system.

Complex PI systems require formal support and maintenance procedures to ensure the overall health of the system. This is where the flexible nature of Agile ends. New increments need a formal process to ensure existing operations and service levels are not impacted. Without a formal process, the risk of failure increases. Using an incremental approach allows a gradual and controlled deployment. In addition, introducing new functionality sooner allows stakeholders to recognize value and lessens the complexity of deployment.

11.5 Summary

The chapter starts with an introduction to the concept of Performance Intelligence (PI). After discussing the characteristics of a PI methodology, the chapter presents an overview of the approaches to a PI project, namely traditional analysis, user-driven, data-driven, data value-chain driven, process-driven, event-driven, object-process driven, joint, goal-driven, model-driven, adaptive business, and agile. In the latter half of the chapter is described the PI delivery framework encompassing discovery, architecture, design, development, test and deployment.

PART IV

PERFORMANCE INTELLIGENCE APPLICATIONS

12
PERFORMANCE
INTELLIGENCE SYSTEMS

This chapter introduces Performance Intelligence Systems (PIS) as constituting of Performance Measurement System (PMS), Corporate Performance Management (CPM) and Business Intelligence (BI). Since we have discussed BI in Chapter 8, this chapter introduces the performance measurement system (PMS) which combines and organizes the performance indicators in order to achieve performance measures. The chapter also explains the corporate performance management (CPM) framework and the CPM commercial solutions available on the market.

A PIS is an important link between *strategic planning* and *operational control*. Traditionally, organizations develop, change, and pursue improvement in two different ways: using a top-down strategy, cascading from top management down throughout the entire organization, or bottom-up with incremental improvement processes promoted from below. Both of these concepts are well integrated with PIS. PIS have evolved from a characterization based on the measurement and control of costs to one that is based on the measurement of value creation, and therefore is also based on noncost performances.

Performance is an integral part of corporate strategy and consists of performance objectives and the means/actions required to achieve them. Performance evaluation is increasingly important, not just in relation to predefined and predetermined standards, but also to support continuous improvement. Measuring and monitoring tools are required to achieve the satisfactory implementation of improvement programs like just-in-time, total quality management, etc., which have their own specific strategies.

12.1 Performance Measurement System

The term "balanced scorecard" was coined by Kaplan and Norton in their famous article published in the *Harvard Business Review* in 1992, the year that many consider the beginning of the introduction and dissemination of PMS worldwide. The balanced scorecard was the particular model of PMS proposed by Kaplan and Norton but is now synonymous with PMS.

The purposes of PMS are:

- The translation and verification of the corporate strategic plan (goals+instruments) and support for intervention improvement programs
- Comparison with the performance of its best competitors (benchmarking)
- The control/monitoring of operational activities
- The coordination of activities
- The evaluation of human resources
- The involvement and motivation of human resources
- Individual and organizational learning (e.g., "learning-by-measure" and "learning by error")

12.1.1 Performance Indicators and Measures

A performance measure is the value assumed by an indicator (of performance). The performance will be *ex ante* an objective of performance and *ex post* a result of performance.

The formalization of measures mainly includes the definition of objects/phenomena to be measured. The next step refers to the study of measurability and definition of the metrics (if the measures are expressed in numerical form) or semantics (if the measures are prevented with lexical attributes, such as excellent, good, fair, etc.).

Formalization of the measures involves:

- Definition of the object or phenomenon to be measured
- Measurability
- Metrics or semantics
- Degree of detail
- Understanding, agreement
- Applicability, significance, uniqueness

- Convenient, essentiality, compatibility
- Performance result responsibility manager
- Performance result user
- Uses

The formalization of process measurements, that is, the processes leading up to the measurement activities, includes the measurement criteria (time, place, and method of identification) and the cost analysis and frequency of recognition

Formalization of the measurement process involves:

- Criteria (moment, place, and method of detection)
- Cost and frequency
- Responsibility
- Precision (repeatability)
- Accuracy (likelihood)
- Completeness
- Timeliness
- Maintainability/adaptability

12.1.2 PMS Architecture

The three different architectures are:

- *Vertical:* This defines the indicators at different organizational levels (operational, tactical, strategic) and how the various indicators relate to each other to form a synthesis.

  With regard to this architecture, there is the problem of obtaining the best synthesis, reducing the number of indicators, but without losing excessive information power.
- *Horizontal:* This defines which are the most suitable indicators for the various organizational units (functions, offices, etc.) and which indicators are communicated/compared between different organizational units.

  With regard to this architecture, there is a problem of different languages/backgrounds in different areas/business functions (e.g., technical production data are not always easy for the sales division to understand and, vice versa, sales data can be difficult for production operators to understand).

- *By processes:* This defines which indicators are able to measure and monitor organizational processes (which by definition cut across organizational functions) and how these are determined by organizational unit and individual resource indicators.

  With regard to the process architecture, there is the problem of the relationship between process performance and the performances of each area/function (i.e., the identification of responsibility manager of a result).

12.1.3 PMS Interfaces

A PMS is not an isolated system partly because it shares input data with other business systems as it also produces outputs for other systems.

A PMS should be integrated with at least three other types of systems:

1. A strategic planning system
2. An accounting or management control system encompassing
   - External accounting
     - Balance sheets
     - Budget analysis
     - Financial flows
   - Internal accounting
     - Cost accounting and analysis of product margins
     - Budgeting further to deviance analysis
     - Evaluation and analysis of investments
3. A production management system
   - Material requirement planning (MRP)
   - Manufacturing planning and control system (MPSC)
     - Master production planning
   - Enterprise resources planning (ERP)
     - Sales management
     - Accounting
     - Treasury Management
     - Asset management
     - Administration
     - Human source modules

12.1.4 PMS Models

Corresponding to the three different architectures, the three PMS models are:

1. Hierarchical models (or top-down), characterized by "cost" and "noncost" performance at different levels of aggregation, until they translate into final results. However, these models do not always manage to summaries all the measures in economic financial results, but the latter can be separated from aggregate measures of customer satisfaction.
2. Balanced scorecard or tableau de bord models, which consider the results separately, that is, they maintain various categories corresponding to different aspects in a horizontal position (financial, operational, customer, innovation, and learning) without aggregating the results.
3. Process-oriented models, starting with those that simply use the distinction between internal and external performance, and those that explicitly consider the processes of an organization and the value chain.

12.2 Corporate Performance Management Framework

12.2.1 Planning and Forecasting

The key process in CPM applications is the integrated planning and multidimensional system which, in addition to covering the different versions of planning documents and different time horizons, also allows for coherent management in sync with the sales budget and rolling forecasts for the period phases, through to the core aspects of economic, financial, and cash flow planning.

Support throughout the entire process must include an appropriate workflow for the dissemination and validation of progress reports, further to the ability to track changes and interventions that the involved actors carry out during work sessions. Short-term budgeting will be integrated within long-term plans, if possible coherently with business plans and the management of strategic initiatives relating to monitoring and performance objectives that will converge as targets on the specific scorecard modules.

12.2.2 Balanced Scorecard and Dashboard

The identification of critical success factors, the allocation of key performance indicators (KPIs), and the aggregation of measures from different areas, rendered consistent by component maps and causal relationships according to the balanced scorecard and value-based management methodologies, is the second process that a CPM environment must be capable of enabling.

Dashboards are important reporting tools that allow for the contextualization of the relevant indicators into fast and intuitive representations full of graphs and diagrams. The structuring of these mechanisms is extremely useful both as a preferential logic input for any type of analysis and investigation and as an effective way of measuring the alignment of objectives between the different corporate areas and responsibilities.

12.2.3 Profitability and Cost Management

Among the various CPM processes, there are also cost allocation and simulation tools for economic and management structures, using the typical drivers adopted during the budgeting phase, activity-based drivers and standard factors, thus eliminating the more limited cost accounting environments.

The inclusion of costing systems such as activity-based costing (ABC), activity-based management (ABM) or other liberal combinations of the traditional techniques are strongly supported by the need of companies to compare their strategic initiatives in terms of profitability and return on investment. No less important is cost optimization and, more importantly, the focus of activities targeted by the product and customer in terms of generated value is now the core objective of all economic sectors.

12.2.4 Group Reporting and Financial Consolidation

An increasing level of importance is now being given not only by corporate groups which control a number of different companies but also by organizations with multiple business units or divisions, to group reporting and financial consolidation, mainly to address the urgency of complying with standards and regulatory requirements that also impose higher levels of transparency and accuracy when drafting interim financial statements.

These applications, in compliance with the generally accepted regulations and principles such as GAAP, IAS/IFRS, and Basel II, make it possible to integrate within the CPM platform, a number of tools to support the activities of internal auditors and contextually facilitate their interaction with independent analysts.

12.3 CPM Software

The analysis conducted annually by Gartner on the CPM suite software manufacturers market, the "Magic Quadrant," highlighted how all players in this sector are trying to complete their offerings by integrating the performance management tools described above into their software solutions. The market is focusing on this aspect and hence the solutions tend to look rather similar; the differences are mainly based on the role that different players pursue and seek to implement in relation to their own dimensions and evolutionary strategies.

The categorization of leaders, visionaries, and experts is also very useful to help understand how operators with different market shares and strategies, identify the distinguishing factors and the winning elements to focus on in order to consolidate their position or gain additional space and visibility.

These elements can provide us with interesting viewpoints on market development; it is clear that in the CPM world, supply inevitably responds to demand, in this case software solution manufacturers who mainly focused on instruments and tools that have led to the realization of successful projects. The success of these applications is, according to these operators, shown by the changes they have generated and the consequent increase in the number of users enabled to implement performance management and control, through the access and interaction provided by the solutions on offer.

Among the many leaders in the market, we have selected vendors who illustrate, for different reasons, the most significant market trends.

12.3.1 SAP Business Objects

With the acquisition of Business Objects and Cartesis, following that of OutlookSoft, SAP pursues the strategy of integrating Business Intelligence and Performance Management modules in its worldwide base of ERP.

The union of two dominant positions in the ERP sector with SAP and the BI sector with Business Objects suggests there will be considerable scope for action with tools that were already leaders in their specific planning, consolidation, vertical analytics, and management reporting fields. The critical point currently seems to be the actual and definitive integration of these solutions into one single platform that guarantees the level of continuity required by efficient CPM processes.

12.3.2 Oracle Hyperion

The acquisition of Hyperion was a highly important move for Oracle who wanted to enter the CPM market with a suitable product considered strategic and complementary to its existing data warehouse and business intelligence management applications.

Oracle declares that, with this acquisition, it intends to consolidate the presence of Hyperion and its Essbase multidimensional database, not just in the planning and consolidation areas, but also by integrating the Enterprise Performance Management (EPM) suite into more extended and dynamic analytic environments, to make it one of the most complete CPM suites.

Given its leadership position and the support services provided, the pricing aspect must be considered by medium-size companies that require architectures for a large number of users.

12.3.3 IBM Cognos

Cognos is an established brand for environments dedicated to planning and management reporting, which has strengthened its position with the continuous development of vertical extensions.

Budgeting and forecasting have always been their best functionality (Planning), and the financial reporting and consolidation (Controller) applications made it possible to complete the CPM functions.

12.3.4 SAS

SAS is currently one of the few of the historical BI solution manufacturers to remain independent. It has always held a strong position in the advanced simulation and predictive analysis area and has maintained its approach in processing information of a strategic nature, providing a wide range of interpretative models, particularly for cost accounting and cause and effect maps.

SAS is highly specialized in the financial and public administration sectors, and seems to be less present in industrial sectors where the availability of very sophisticated models makes it difficult to reconcile its cost with the budgets of small to medium size manufacturing companies.

12.3.5 Microsoft

When Microsoft declares its intention to enter a market, other competitors must pay attention, especially because of the competitive advantages it has in terms of pricing, integration with the ubiquitous Office environment, and its countless global technological partnerships.

The Analytics Microsoft suite now has all the components of a CPM platform, although it has only a limited presence in corporate environments. The attractiveness of the reporting environments and the familiarity of the analysis environments generate a high level of interest among controlling staff, who usually handle huge volumes of Excel spreadsheets.

Its current level of integration with non-Microsoft IT sources seems to restrict its adoption by organizations that have consolidated their use of different architectures over the years.

12.4 CPM Project Enablers

Analysis of the elements characterizing technology leaders indicates the most critical steps toward a an effective CPM program mainly depend on the coherence of organizational and project decisions with the Performance Management objectives the firm wishes to achieve.

Companies frequently have an excessive amount of data and indicators. Often this information is inconsistent and is not related by causal relationships to the measurement indicators of their current action plans. The real challenge is therefore to select and then align the different measures with the Performance Management methodology it intends to adopt. Otherwise there is the risk that line managers will continue to use their own measures and yardsticks.

There are four key requirements that cannot be ignored when creating a CPM project and that must be met and resolved to suit different business environments.

1. Metrics Definition

   The definition of corporate metrics is an activity with significant impact or ramifications, and the discussions and results obtained during the identification and development of relationships between the different KPIs is a critical process, regardless of the subsequent realization stages. The metabase that it establishes becomes the center and sole reference of the required functional extensions that would allow the CPM to interact with the various business areas using a common language.

   Management starts by formalizing clear objectives and key action plans in order to allocate the process ownership and initially define the key aspects to monitor. The key at this stage lies in the highest possible level of sharing all KPIs. If the metrics are not aligned with the objectives, the objectives are not aligned with the strategies, and the strategies are not communicated to those responsible for their achievement, it is almost certain that the targets achieved will be very disappointing. This is why these indicators cannot be imposed from above or from independent experts, but in order to achieve the objective for which they were defined, the alignment of strategies and actions, they must be the result of a circular pathway, adjoined with subsequent review and refinement phases.

2. Cause–Effect Maps and Relationships

   Companies that do not develop their CPM project using a coherent map of the main components of the business and their mutual impacts and cause–effect diagrams, such as the balanced scorecard, cannot expect to achieve a result other than the mere display of a list of KPIs.

Obtaining a series, however large, of indicators that are only vaguely linked or, in some cases, even incoherent, will cause the exact opposite result compared to that expected; in fact, the series will actually complicate the understanding of phenomena without being able to detect the drivers and possible improvement actions.

3. Modeling Data Management

CPM projects are easier to implement for those companies that already have a solid data warehouse architecture. This simplifies the integration of different information sources, aggregation by significant dimensions, and, above all, research for the most reliable and useful data according to a specific need.

In fact, a considerable amount of effort required to execute a scorecard project concerns the complexity of the data search, to find the data most consistent with the indicator structure to be realized and at the same time the easiest to retrieve and make available.

The support of process managers is crucial in order to include the CPM within business activities and thereby consolidate strategy and performance management. They are the persons responsible for the translation of guidelines and targets in business process management.

The best way to achieve consensus and the resulting alignment of conduct, is to allow for the depth of analysis that also satisfies the monitoring and planning requirements in different areas of responsibility.

12.5 Summary

This chapter introduced the performance measurement system (PMS). A PMS combines and organizes the performance indicators in order to achieve performance measures. The chapter explained the corporate performance management (CPM) framework, and the CPM commercial solutions available on the market, namely SAP Business Objects, Oracle Hyperion, IBM Cognos, SAS, and Microsoft.

13

BALANCE SCORECARD
SYSTEMS

13.1 Balance Scorecard (BSC)

A company's emphasis is not on acquiring the latest technology per se, because that will change in the future too, but rather on confronting any changes in the market with a strategy that will help customers continue to value the company's products and services while also differentiating them more effectively from those provided by competitors. This is the subtle reason why a few years ago General Motor's much known foray into highly automated manufacturing facilities to beat the Japanese on productivity and quality was not very successful. Thus, a company needs a management system to assess and evaluate its strategy in terms of competitiveness and performance in the future. There is also the important need for the company to be able to dynamically monitor the progress and performance of the execution of these strategies, which will then enable the company to administer any corrections or adjustments based on the real-time operational feedback received from such a system. The balance scorecard (BSC) is precisely such a strategic management system that enables an enterprise to monitor and manage the execution of its value-adding and value-creating strategies effectively. Enterprises also need an information systems that can empower them to implement the BSC.

The BSC aims to provide a balance between the external and internal measures of performance, between short- and long-term objectives, between financial and nonfinancial measures, and between lagging and leading indicators. It is not limited to being merely a measurement and control system, but has actually developed over the course of time into a full-featured management system for the successful implementation of a company's strategy.

The BSC provides companies with a framework for translating the company's vision and strategy into a coherent set of performance measures. It derives the objectives and measures of the value determinants or the corresponding performance drivers based on the vision and strategy of the company. As shown in Figure 13.1, the BSC framework consists of the following four perspectives:

- Financial
- Customer
- Internal business processes
- Learning and growth

The BSC retains the financial perspective of the company's performance that is essentially based on past performance and is valid for short-term performance in the immediate future. However, it supplements this traditional perspective with those of the customer and the internal system, process, and people who determine the company's value-generating potential and hence long-term financial performance in the future. The customer's perspective ensures the continual relevance of the products and services provided by the company. The internal perspective of business processes and the people ensures that the company surpasses the customer's expectations on critical value

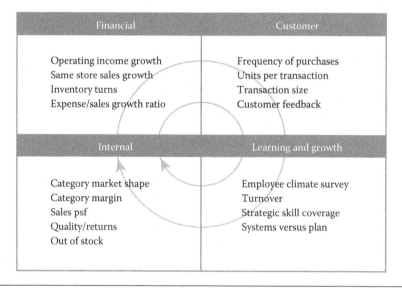

Figure 13.1 The Balance Scorecard (BSC) framework.

determinants like quality, timeliness, innovation, and service. It is in this sense that the BSC represents a balance between the external value determinants of the customers and shareholders, and the corresponding internal value drivers of the critical systems, business processes, and people.

Two kinds of value drivers exist: outcome and performance. Outcome drivers are lagging indicators like financial measures that are objective, quantifiable, and past-facing. On the other hand, performance measures are leading indicators that link with the company's strategy and provide the rationale for the achievements of the outcome drivers. Although performance drivers are future-facing, the impact and effectiveness of performance drivers on the outcome measures is highly subjective. This is compensated by the dynamic nature of the BSC system that treats evaluation and feedback as an important element of the framework. The value drivers are constantly under test for continued relevance in the market and any deviations observed in the customer's value determinants are immediately cascaded in terms of the changes in the value drivers' measures or the value drivers themselves. This corresponds to the learning and growth perspective of the BSC framework. It represents the capability of institutional learning, which is the powerful concept of *double-loop* learning.

In fact, the entire BSC framework is based on a perceived cause-and-effect relationship between the various strategies, organizational elements, and processes of the enterprise. It is in the context of these assumptions that the BSC also incorporates the cause-and-effect relationships in terms of the relationships between the various outcome and performance drivers. For instance, the Return on Capital Employed (ROCE) driver (in the financial perspective) is dependent on customer loyalty (in the customer perspective). Customer loyalty is dependent on the enterprise's product quality and responsiveness (in the internal business processes perspective), which in turn is dependent on the minimization of product defects, knowledge of the customer's prior transaction history, recorded preferences, and so on (learning and growth perspective). It is because of this that the multiple objectives and measures of the BSC do not entail complex trade-offs but can easily be integrated into a consistent framework of 20–25 value drivers that can help navigate the strategy of the company successfully through the turbulent marketplace.

The strategic management of enterprises using the BSC involves the following stages:

1. Mapping the company strategy into the BSC framework in terms of the strategic objectives and drivers for the BSC. This might also involve reconciling or prioritizing among various objectives or defining differing objectives and drivers for different divisions. This stage identifies all processes that are critical to the strategic performance of the enterprise. It must be noted that the BSC is a methodology for implementing a company strategy and not for formulating one. This is another reason why it is highly suitable for incorporating it into the SAP SEM solution.

2. Communicating the link between the strategic objectives and measures throughout the enterprise at all levels. This might also involve operationalizing the defined set of measures to the specifics of the local circumstances for the various departmental and functional units of the company. BSCs are usually defined at the level of strategic business units (SBUs), but for a multidivisional company, the defined BSC might incline more toward the financial perspective.

3. Setting targets, devising aligned strategic initiatives, and planning/scheduling initiatives to achieve a breakthrough performance. This might also include financial planning and budgeting as an integrated part of the BSC. From the customer's perspective, this step should include the requirements of both existing and potential customers.

4. Enhancing performance through feedback and learning, based on operational data and reviews. This might entail reprioritizing or changing the performance thresholds or even the value drivers themselves. The latter might become necessary either because of the changes in the marketplace or because the selected set of value drivers might be ineffectual.

Figure 13.2 shows the BSC approach to create a strategy-focused organization.

In the BSC framework, the financial perspective enables a reality check of the strategic management activity of the enterprise. This is because all strategic initiatives meant for improving quality, flexibility, and customer satisfaction might not necessarily translate into improved

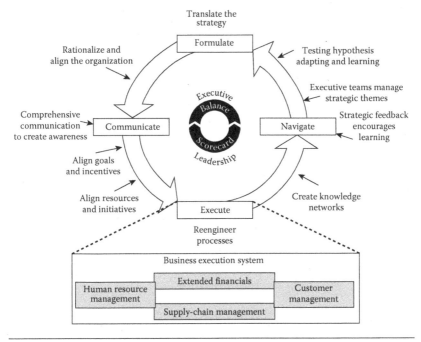

Figure 13.2   BSC approach to create a strategy-focused company.

financial results. If the improved operational outcome as seen from the other three perspectives defined by the company does not end in improved financial results, it might be a powerful indicator of the need for reformulation of the strategy itself. All cause-and-effect relationships that knit a BSC program together must eventually link to financial objectives. Therefore, the financial perspective is preeminent among all perspectives of the BSC framework.

13.1.1 Financial Perspective

As mentioned above, the financial performance measures indicate whether a company's strategy, implementation, and execution are translating into bottom-line financial results. Depending on the business strategy, the financial objectives could be in terms of:

- ROCE, economic value added (EVA), or operating income, and maintaining the market share
- Rapid sales growth and increased market share
- Maximize the generation of cash flow

13.1.2 *Customer Perspective*

The customer perspective mainly addresses the customer- and market-oriented strategies that would deliver improved financial results. This involves the identification of the market segments of interest, the value propositions for each of these segments, and the measures that would help in ascertaining the performance of the company in the selected segments.

The basic outcome measures for this perspective could be

- Customer acquisition
- Customer satisfaction
- Customer retention
- Customer profitability

13.1.3 *Internal Business Processes Perspective*

The internal business processes perspective provides a focus on the business processes that are critical to the success of the enterprise. These processes selected for improvement could be existing processes or could be entirely new processes conceived as a consequence of the strategy of the company. For instance, an excellent example of such a process could be provision for the Web-based procurement of a company's goods and services.

13.1.4 *Learning and Growth Perspective*

The learning and growth perspective addresses the need to build and maintain an appropriate infrastructure for the long-term growth and success of the company. Contributions from the other perspectives, especially regarding envisaged shifts in customer value, might identify the technologies and products essential to the continued relevance of the company's offerings in the marketplace. These contributions might encompass the following:

- People's skills
- Information and support systems
- Organizational processes and procedures

This perspective comprehensively covers employee-related issues like employee satisfaction, employee training, advancement and promotion policies, employee-friendly policies and procedures, productivity-multiplying application environments, and so forth.

13.2 Implementing a BSC

The following section describes how a company might use the Balanced Scorecard to measure the impact of PI as part of its overall organizational performance. The reason for the implementation of the performance measures and related reporting in the financial services company was to support the strategic initiatives of the company. Their stated strategy was to become "customer intimate" and offer "tailored client solutions" for the purposes of obtaining a better understanding of the customer and offering products and services that are tailored to customer needs, thus building stronger customer relationships. The company believed that achievement of these goals would lead to long-term sustainable profits.

The first step in the balanced scorecard process is to articulate the strategy and develop a strategy map. The strategy map identifies the hypothesized strategic linkages between the four key perspectives: financial, customer, internal, and learning and growth.

A strategy map supporting the organization's stated strategy is shown in Figure 13.3.

Having identified the financial objective of long-term sustainable profits and the customer value proposition of providing tailored client solutions and customer intimacy, the strategy map then must focus on the internal processes necessary for the strategy to succeed. The financial services company noted that they needed to develop an understanding of who their "good" customers were so that they could offer product solutions geared toward profitable customers.

The three processes identified were:

- Understanding customer segments
- Developing new products to meet customer needs
- Cross-selling products.

The learning and growth component of the scorecard identifies the need to have improved access to strategic information. This requires the implementation of the information technology infrastructure,

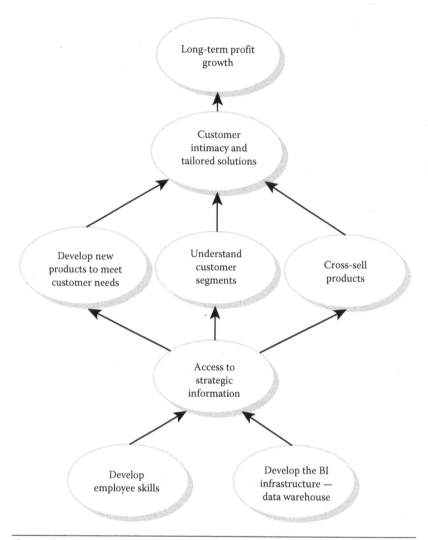

Figure 13.3 Strategy map.

the data warehouse, and related decision support tools for query and analysis. In addition, development of the technical skills necessary to implement, maintain, and support the data warehouse are critical steps in achieving the linked goals of the organization.

Having articulated the strategy and identified the strategized linkages to achieve the strategy, the company must then identify the performance measures that will enable the company to assess whether the goals and objectives have been met.

1. For the financial perspective, the goal of long-term sustainable profitability can be measured through traditional financial measures such as revenue growth, profit growth, revenue mix, and return on investment.
2. For the customer perspective, the objective of attaining tailored client solutions can be measured through customer retention rates, measures of the depth of customer relationships (number of accounts and services used per customer), and customer satisfaction surveys.
3. For the achievement of the internal business processes perspective, the goal of understanding customer segments can be assessed through the use of various metrics such as customer profitability, share of market segment, revenue from new products, and length of the product development cycle.
4. For the achievement of the learning and growth perspective, the objectives can be measuring by examining measures such as access to information technology tools and data, system availability, response times, employee skills assessments, and employee satisfaction surveys. The objectives and performance measures are summarized in Table 13.1.

Table 13.1 Balance Scorecard

BALANCED SCORECARD PERSPECTIVE	OBJECTIVES	STRATEGIC MEASURES
Financial	Long-term sustainable profitability	Revenue growth Profit growth Revenue mix Return on investment
Customer	Tailored customer solutions	Customer retention rates Depth of customer, relationships (# accounts per customer, # services per customer) Customer satisfaction
Internal	Understanding customer segments	Profit by customer segment Share of market segment Revenue from new products Length of the product development cycle
Learning and growth	Development of information systems and employee skills	Access to information technology tools and data System availability IT response times Employee skills assessments Employee satisfaction surveys

13.3 Summary

This chapter presented the balance scorecard (BSC) that provides companies with a framework for translating the company's vision and strategy into a coherent set of performance measures. It describes how based on the vision and strategy of the company, BSC derives the objectives and measures of the value determinants or the corresponding performance drivers in the four constituting perspectives of BSC, namely, financial, customer, internal business processes and, learning and growth.

14

PERFORMANCE INTELLIGENCE FOR THE REAL-TIME ENTERPRISE

The operating contexts of enterprises have changed internally and externally during the last decades. For instance, direct costs shrank, indirect costs increased drastically, and the product portfolio has more variants. As a result, the traditional performance metrics are inadequate to monitor and control the manufacturing processes. Numerous performance measurement systems (PMSs) have evolved, which stress the importance of financial and nonfinancial/operational metrics, and the alignment of financial metrics and operational metrics with the enterprise objectives. Overall, these systems provide a comprehensive overview of an enterprise to sustain competitive advantage.

The financial and operational metrics are two sides of the same coin—both are essential for monitoring and controlling manufacturing processes. A resource is an entity that is common between the financial and operational metrics. A resource has well-defined processing capabilities and throughput capacities. These capabilities and capacity of a resource are employed during the execution of manufacturing processes generating process data in real time. The process data provide awareness about different enterprise entities including products, resources and production orders, customers, and so on.

Enterprise applications, especially enterprise resource planning (ERP) systems, store context information or transactional data about enterprise entities. The acquisition of process data in real time and the corresponding transactional data can be used to simultaneously compute the financial and operational metrics in real time. Consequently, a comprehensive view of an enterprise can be presented to different audiences by converting the lagging financial metrics into leading financial metrics, and link the financial and operational metrics in real time.

After introducing the real-time enterprise (RTE), this chapter discusses the various aspects involved in instituting and servicing financial and operational metrics for a RTE. It introduces an event-driven framework for monitoring and controlling manufacturing processes for the RTE. The chapter also presents a representative reference architecture for enabling real-time performance measurements involving different fundamentals, technologies, and standards.

14.1 Real-Time Enterprise

The RTE is a vision to manage an enterprise in (near) real time. The vision of an RTE addresses the necessity to cope with time in a comprehensive way; thus, RTE as an enterprise competes by using up-to-date-information to progressively remove delays to the management and execution of its critical business processes. The RTE monitors, captures, and analyzes root cause and overt events that are critical to its success the instant those events occur, to identify new opportunities, avoid mishaps, and minimize delays in core business processes. The presentation and discussions in this chapter are adapted from S. Karadgi (2014) and D. Metz (2014).

RTE basic principles are:

1. Realization of capabilities to satisfy individualized customer demands
2. Automation of value creation processes
3. Integration of IT systems across enterprise borders
   Characteristics of RTE are:
   a. Information has to be acquired automatically at the point-of-creation (POC) from IT systems (e.g., ERP), programmable logic controllers (PLC), radio frequency identification (RFID) chips, and so on.
   b. Information created at the POC is immediately accessible at the point-of-action (POA) for decision-making. This requires the realization of seamless information flows in (near) real-time. Applying publish–subscribe communication patterns seems to be promising to realize such information flows.

c. A real-time system has to select relevant information that should be made accessible at the POA. Acquired data at the POC has to be filtered, aggregated, and delivered in an adequate timeframe (e.g., seconds, minutes, hours). Thus, only a significant subset of all state variables has to be made available for control purposes.

d. There should be no breaks in semantics across various IT systems. Hence, the consideration of standards (e.g., ontologies) regarding data semantics is recommended.

e. The decision-making in RTE can be performed at the POA without human interactions or at least with minimum human assistance.

In addition to individualization as well as automation, enterprise integration has to be achieved or appropriately addressed in an RTE. Thus, in addition to horizontal integration of an enterprise with its external environment, the vertical enterprise integration across enterprise levels, which is capable of linking planned and actual process execution, is a prerequisite for the realization of an RTE in manufacturing. At the strategic level, the enterprise's external environment is delineated as SCM and CRM, and their horizontal integration with the enterprise is understood as the extended enterprise. At the tactical level, administrative, purchasing, and financial processes are executed. The actual value creation is performed at the resource level or manufacturing level.

An enterprise is considered as being composed of several hierarchical levels. At each level, certain functions are executed, and information is processed and exchanged between adjacent levels:

1. Level 4 is concerned with *business planning and logistics*, and is performed on time frames of months, weeks, and days.

2. Level 3 activities are concerned with *scheduling* manufacturing execution system (MES) and operates on time frames of days, shifts, hours, minutes, and seconds, and make up the MES (e.g., detailed scheduling, dispatching production).

3. Level 2 activities *monitor and control* the physical processes in hours, minutes, seconds, or even faster. The aim of level 0 to level 2 is to bring/maintain the process to/in stable condition.

4. Level 1 is about activities for *sensing and manipulating* the physical processes, thus operates in (milli-) seconds. Typically, this

level encompasses sensors and actuators known for automation systems.

5. Level 0 describes the *actual physical processes*, which are manufacturing processes in the context of this research work.

Figure 14.1 shows the manufacturing execution system (MES) model. The vertical integration of a manufacturing enterprise across the various enterprise levels is challenging as they are associated with different time horizons varying from (milli-) seconds over hours and days to quarters and years. In other words, business processes located at the tactical level are predominantly executed *offline*, whereas manufacturing processes situated at the shop floor level are executed *online*. Consequently, these characteristics of the enterprise levels result in a semantic and temporal vertical integration gap.

MESs are located at the manufacturing control level and try to bridge the vertical integration gap. However, inflexible and proprietary interfaces between shop-floor resources and enterprise applications (e.g., ERP system) impede a seamless vertical integration. These shortcomings are addressed by employing the Service Oriented Architecture (SOA) paradigm at the manufacturing level.

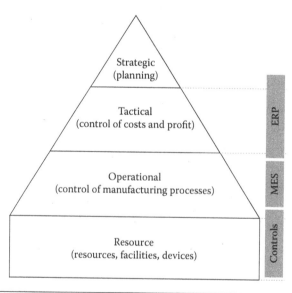

Figure 14.1 Manufacturing execution system (MES) model.

Eleven functions of the control domain for MES level 3 are:

1. *Resource allocation and control* is about the management of resources including machines, tools, labor skills, and the like. It especially encompasses the reservation of resources in accordance with the production schedule. Further, resources' status is gathered in real time and detailed history of resource usage is provided.

2. Based on prescribed production schedules, *dispatching of production* is responsible for the management of production flow with regard to jobs, production orders, batches, lots, and so on. Here, it is also envisaged that the production schedule can be adapted within agreed limits and in (near) real time in case of the occurrence of certain events (e.g., resource breakdown).

3. The *collection and acquisition of data* concerning production equipment and manufacturing processes is a prerequisite for other functionalities.

4. The control of product quality by a (near) real-time provision of quality data (measurements) gathered from manufacturing and analysis is part of *quality management*. Quality management may derive (re-) actions to mitigate quality problems and ensure adherence of manufactured products to corresponding product specifications. The functionality often includes statistical process control (SPC) or statistical quality control (SQC).

5. *Process management* monitors manufacturing processes and automatically corrects or improves in-process functions. The corrected or improved in-process functions can be either:
   a. *Intra-operational*, thus are focused on certain machines or equipment
   b. *Inter-operational*, and thus address the overall manufacturing process
   Process management encompasses alarm management to inform personnel about process deviations.

6. *Product tracking* provides status information about personnel, materials, production conditions, alarms, and the like that are related to a product. Forward and backward traceability are

available if the aforementioned status information is recorded for a product, which can be retrieved at a later point in time.

7. *Performance analysis* provides up-to-the-minute information about resource utilization, actual cycle times, conformance to production schedule, and the like. The actual performance values can also be contrasted with past and expected performance values.

8. The *operations and detailed scheduling* functionality is in charge of deriving a sequence of (production) orders based on priorities, characteristics, and production rules. Also, the sequencing considers actual and finite resource capacities.

9. *Document control* encompasses the control of documents, such as recipes, drawings, shift-to-shift communication, and so on.

10. The provision of up-to-the-minute status information about personnel as well as attendance reporting, certification tracking, and so on is part of *labor management*.

11. *Maintenance management* ensures the functioning and availability of production resources (e.g., machines, tools). It encompasses planned (i.e., periodic or preventive) and urgent maintenance activities.

The RTE's goal of a comprehensive real-time control of performance of manufacturing processes necessitates the examination of shop-floor events with respect to their administrative and financial context.

Accordingly, the *necessary* condition of the RTE is the basic vertical integration of enterprise data, and the *sufficient* condition of the RTE is the event processing and (automatic) deduction of appropriate (re-) actions.

14.2 Real-Time Performance Measurement

The operating scenarios of enterprises have changed internally and externally during the last decades. For instance, direct costs shrank, indirect costs increased drastically, and the product portfolio has more variants. As a result, the traditional performance metrics were inadequate to monitor and control the manufacturing processes.

The traditional financial metrics were insufficient to manage the changes in the external and internal environments:

- These metrics solely concentrated on internal processes with the objective of minimizing the unit cost of a product and variance.
- Managers had a retrospective view of an enterprise as the financial metrics were derived offline (e.g., monthly and quarterly), and hence these metrics are considered as laggards.
- The metrics did not provide any valuable insight into the processes that can be used as inputs for decision-making and process improvement programs, among others.
- The financial metrics greatly encouraged the achievement of short-term objectives, did not guide in the realization of the enterprise's strategy, and favored local optimization of processes.

Numerous PMSs have evolved, which stress the importance of financial and nonfinancial/operational metrics, and the alignment of financial metrics and operational metrics with the enterprise objectives. The systems include Performance Pyramid System, Balanced Scorecard, Performance Prism and European Foundation for Quality Management (EFQM) Excellence Model, and so on.

Accountants have difficulties in consolidating operational metrics. The financial metrics are expressed using currency that is extremely aggregated and conceals the operational details; similarly, in most of the cases, the financial metrics cannot be easily traced to products and production orders. In contrast, the operational metrics are communicated as an index, which represents efficient and effective use of raw materials and resources, among others. Along with the advances in PMSs, the traditional accounting techniques have evolved from pure allocation of costs to trace and assign costs based on causal relationships. In this regard, the notable accounting techniques are the following:

- Activity-based costing (ABC)
- Resource consumption accounting (RCA)

The financial metrics are considered as lagging metrics as they are calculated according to the enterprise's reporting cycle, that is, offline.

Consequently, this will lead to realizing a sluggish closed-loop feedback cycle. The improvement associated with the real time or online monitoring and control of manufacturing processes can be enhanced if the closed-loop feedback cycle consists of real-time financial metrics. The real-time financial metrics must be linked with the corresponding operational metrics in real time, and plant managers and supervisors have access to these metrics in reasonable amount of time, more specifically in real time.

The operational metrics are treated as leading metrics as they are computed in real time or online, which enable to take necessary reactive or proactive actions to minimize deviations from planned values/objectives, and support future planning and decision-making based on facts. MES support in the following:

- Automated collection and aggregation of process data
- Computation of operational metrics
- Timely display of operational metrics to enterprise members to initiate suitable actions

Subsequently, this enables realization of real time or online monitoring and control of manufacturing processes employing shorter closed-loop feedback cycle. In comparison to the offline monitoring and control of manufacturing processes, this will result in around 10%–20% improvements in performance via increased throughput, reduced cycle time, improved quality, and so on.

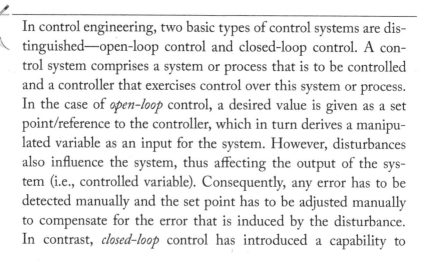

In control engineering, two basic types of control systems are distinguished—open-loop control and closed-loop control. A control system comprises a system or process that is to be controlled and a controller that exercises control over this system or process. In the case of *open-loop* control, a desired value is given as a set point/reference to the controller, which in turn derives a manipulated variable as an input for the system. However, disturbances also influence the system, thus affecting the output of the system (i.e., controlled variable). Consequently, any error has to be detected manually and the set point has to be adjusted manually to compensate for the error that is induced by the disturbance. In contrast, *closed-loop* control has introduced a capability to automatically compensate for the disturbance in the system. The output of the system is measured (i.e., controlled variable) and a feedback signal/value is sent to a comparator. In most instances, the comparator calculates the difference between the desired value (set point) and the feedback (i.e., negative feedback). This difference is called an *error* and is fed into the controller that calculates a manipulated variable, which will effectively reduce future errors. Thus, the system is set to achieve a state of balance or equilibrium.

14.2.1 Activity-Based Costing

ABC concentrates mainly on activities performed in an enterprise. An activity is identified as work performed by people, equipment, technologies, or facilities. Per the activity-based cost management resource framework, costs are assigned to activities depending upon the consumption of resources by the activities, and these activity costs are reassigned to cost object (e.g., products, processes) based on cause-and-effect relationships and proportional use of activities. The ABC system can be employed in an enterprise manufacturing heterogeneous mix of products, namely standard and custom products, low-volume products, high-volume products, and mature products.

ABC management framework consists of the process view and the assignment view. The activities are horizontally linked as processes and sub-processes along the process view that are necessary to fulfill the requirements of production orders. The cost assignment view consists of three cost drivers, namely resource, activity, and cost object, and two cost assignments, namely resource cost and activity cost. The resource cost assignment is used to link a resource and the activities performed by it. A resource driver traces expenditures (cash outlay) to work activities; it quantitatively measures the amount of a resource used by an activity. An activity driver traces activity costs to cost objects. For example, machine hours, production runs, maintenance hours, setup hours are activity drivers; it quantitatively measures the output of an activity. The activity cost assignment is employed to assign activity costs to a cost object based on the consumption of an activity.

ABC system has not been adapted widely, primarily because of its complexity. The definition of activities and associated cost drivers, in most cases, is subjective being based on the enterprise members' role(s), responsibility(ies), and experience. Furthermore, managing the activity list is expensive and difficult as the model size increases exponentially. Consequently, it is absolutely necessary to trade off the accuracy of the generated cost information against the effort to maintain the ABC system.

A simplified and more popular form of ABC system called time-driven activity-based costing (TDABC) requires two input parameters for an activity—the capacity cost rate of supplying a resource and the capacity usage of the resource by products, service, and customers, which are multiplied to derive the cost information.

14.2.2 Resource Consumption Accounting

RCA stresses the importance of the process view to manage the activities. RCA technique is built around recourses and not activities; the capacity, capabilities, and costs reside in resources. The resources with similar characteristics and outputs, among others, are grouped together in a resource pool; the cause-and-effect relationships are realized by resource drivers and activity drivers. In contrast to ABC, these drivers are quantity based, indicating quantity of resource (pool) output consumed, with the understanding that costs follow quantity.

RCA stresses the importance of the inherent nature of cost. This initial nature of cost is reflected in primary fixed and proportional costs, which are incurred at a resource. Likewise, the changing nature of cost is reflected in secondary fixed and proportional costs during the consumption of resource outputs. Overall, the interrelationships between resources and the corresponding quantity flows, that is, underlying nature of costs are crucial. The fixed costs are computed based on the theoretical capacity of a resource pool and are not assigned (purely) based on the consumption of resource outputs. In contrast, proportional costs are assigned based on the consumption of resource outputs. Likewise, there are quantities that can be treated as fixed and proportional. Overall, the aforementioned costs and quantities along with the resource output quantity are used to derive the resource unit rate.

RCA presents managers with detailed and accurate information about resource quantity consumption with the ability to carry out variance analysis at the resource level. This assists in managing planned and theoretical capacity, especially the identification of excess/idle capacity.

14.3 Events

An event can be described as anything that changes the status in some way and can be represented as a change of a *state*.

An event object encompasses the following three aspects:

1. Event form indicates the data associated with an event and are also known as event attributes. The data can be a combination of simple and complex data types, and timestamps [108], which can originate from multiple sources.
2. Event significance denotes an activity/operation and the corresponding data associated with the activity is represented by the event form.
3. Event relativity describes the relationships with other events.

In manufacturing scenarios, an event form can be represented by manufacturing activity parameters (e.g., temperature and spindle speed), event significance denotes manufacturing activity (e.g., milling), and event relativity identifies the relationship of a manufacturing activity with the product and production order.

Events are triggered randomly, which necessitates establishing relationships between events to realize real-time monitoring and control of manufacturing processes. There exist different types of relationships between events, which are possibly based on time, causality, and aggregation.

Events can be simple or complex. A complex event is defined as an event that summarizes, represents, or denotes a set of other events; complex events can be further categorized as derived and composite events based on the methods employed to create these events. An event abstraction is defined as the relationship between a complex event and the other events that it denotes, summarizes, or otherwise represents. Event patterns can create events with higher abstraction levels: the events are arranged hierarchically according to their abstraction level. The event hierarchies establish vertical causality relationships between events across different abstraction levels, while horizontal causality establishes relationships between events in a particular abstraction level.

The sequence of incoming events is known as event stream and can be defined as a linearly ordered sequence of events.

14.3.1 Event-Driven Architecture

Event-driven architecture (EDA) can be defined as an architectural style in which components are event driven and communicate by means of events. Identification, broadcasting, processing, and utilization of events can be realized by employing different components—event producer, event consumers, event processors, event reactions, and messaging backbone.

Event producer is a component in which the events originate and are responsible for publishing events; event producers take different forms. For instance, event producers can be software programs or temperature sensors in a machine. An event contains data that might or might not originate at event producers. Events are pushed to multiple event listeners; event listeners receive only subsets of events in which they are interested. Event listeners can also be event producers. Event listeners can also function as event processors that analyze incoming events. The event reactions can be a combination of the following:

- do nothing
- displaying warning messages
- initiating predefined actions
- triggering new events.

The components of EDA communicate via a messaging backbone, communication mechanism, or an event channel.

14.3.2 Complex Event Processing

In an event cloud, different types of events along with their relationships and abstractions are available for processing. Complex event processing (CEP) is characterized by event capture, event analysis, and event response based on sense–analyze–respond paradigm.

Event patterns which are encoded in a software module as event processing agents (EPAs) are critical for realizing event processing. EPAs have the capability to perform different computations on events, like filtering, aggregating, and deleting event patterns, or filtering, matching, and derivation.

EPAs can be organized into networks and they communicate with each other using the event channel to form event processing networks (EPNs); EPNs can be nested and recursive to represent the complex manufacturing processes. Event processing software loads the EPAs and EPNs into computer memory and processes the incoming events from the event cloud. Event reactions are described as the (re-)action to be taken whenever an event pattern is matched or a predefined situation is detected and is defined in event pattern rules or event pattern–triggered reactive rules.

A unified event management system is based on the publish/subscribe paradigm to deal with primitive and complex events for monitoring.

CEP systems interpret incoming information as notifications of events and focus on detecting relevant patterns among such streaming notifications. In contrast, data stream management systems (DSMSs) focus on transforming the incoming streams of information into new streams, e.g., by joining or aggregating data items.

14.4 Reference Architecture

A reference architecture to materialize many of the functionalities of MES is shown in Figure 14.2.

The resources on the shop floor use different standards and proprietary communication protocols to communicate with other resources and manufacturing management systems. Subsequent data collection provides a modular approach to manage the heterogeneous communication protocols of resources and delivers process data in real time.

The real-time process data delivered by data collection is handled by data aggregation. The real-time process data are assigned to suitable enterprise entities along with the corresponding transactional data from enterprise applications, especially from the ERP system.

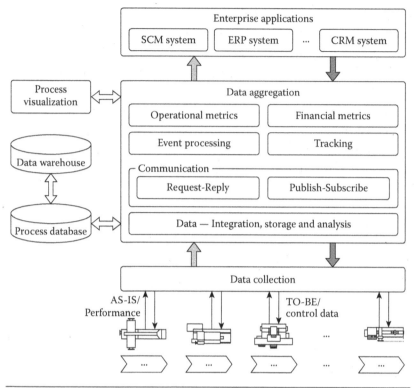

Figure 14.2 A reference architecture for real-time performance measurement.

These data would be referred to as integrated process data, which are managed simultaneously in the following two ways:

1. The integrated data are stored in a process database for offline analysis.
2. The subset of integrated data is employed to realize tracking of enterprise entities in real time.

Tracking is a prerequisite for real-time monitoring and control of manufacturing processes that can be achieved by employing the state-of-the-art event processing techniques. Tracking information is also employed to determine real-time operational and financial metrics.

14.5 Financial Metrics

From the context of financial metrics, instead of monitoring and control, performance analysis, and planning and decision-making are used. The production performance information which flows from production control to product cost accounting is related to the actual consumption of raw materials, labor hours, energy, and resources (i.e., AS-IS values). This information can be identified with products, coproducts, and scrap. The product cost accounting is involved with the computation of total product costs, reporting on production costs, and setting future cost objectives (i.e., TO-BE values).

The product cost accounting functionality is part of level 4 and is supported by the ERP system, may be in coordination with other enterprise applications, such as the SCM system. The outcome of product cost accounting is further aggregated to derive numerous financial metrics. Overall, the financial metrics are highly aggregated, that is, operational details, product and production complexity, and production disturbances, among others are suppressed or not highlighted.

These financial metrics are calculated offline according to the enterprise's reporting cycle. The computed metrics are delivered late, and the performance evaluation, planning, and decision-making processes are temporally delayed. At the end, decisions taken will not match the current manufacturing situations. Thus, it is necessary to have a narrow perspective of product cost accounting at the manufacturing control level to accurately compute, especially in real time, costs surrounding manufacturing in contrast to the broader perspective of ERP systems toward product cost accounting

14.6 Operational Metrics

It is indispensable to compute the operational metrics in real time to enhance monitoring and control of manufacturing processes. Process analysis and modeling is crucial in order to identify operational metrics, relationships, and dependencies between operational metrics and the data required to compute them.

After computation, the operational metrics will be forwarded to the data aggregation component. Subsequently, the computed operational metrics will be used in numerous ways. Firstly, the operational metrics are forwarded to all subscribed process visualization clients for displaying those using visual elements, such as charts and gauges.

The process visualization clients also consider the roles and responsibilities of the enterprise members. Secondly, the operational metrics are analyzed by the event processing component. This component is in charge of aligning the enterprise processes according to the planned objectives. Finally, the performance measures are stored in the process database for creating reports.

14.7 Summary

This chapter discussed the various aspects involved in instituting and servicing financial and operational metrics for a RTE. For monitoring and controlling manufacturing processes for the RTE, it introduced an event-driven framework consisting of events, EDA, and CEP. The chapter also presented a representative reference architecture for enabling real-time performance measurements involving different fundamentals, technologies, and standards

Epilogue

Intelligence Maturity Model

Table E.1 presents the intelligence maturity model (IMM).

E.1 Data

Data have experienced a variety of definitions, largely depending on the context of their use. For example, Information Science defines data as unprocessed information and other domains treat data as a representation of objective facts. Data result from representation of facts, observation, or an event. Data are understood as discrete, atomistic, tiny packets that have no inherent structure or necessary relationship between them. They are discrete; they can be piled-up, captured, and retrieved, or be recorded and manipulated.

Table E.1   Intelligence Maturity Model

Data	-	Data file
Communication	Metadata	Data tables, mapping, and transformation
Information	Meaning	Databases, indices, and spreadsheets
Intelligence	Analytics	Data warehouses, OLAPs
Knowledge	Context	Knowledge bases
Wisdom	Heuristics	Expert systems

Data are recorded (captured and stored) symbols and signal readings: symbols include words (text and/or verbal), numbers, diagrams, and images (still and/or video), which are the building blocks of communication; signals include sensor and/or sensory readings of light, sound, smell, taste, and touch. As symbols, "Data" are the storage of intrinsic meaning, a mere representation. The main purpose of data is to record activities or situations, to attempt to capture the true picture or the real event.

Data are a measuring unit of cognition that describes transactions between natural, artificial, or semantic systems. In businesses, data can measure performance characteristics of production, distribution, transportation, or service.

E.2 Communication

Communication is a method of transmission from a generating source to receiving destination. Communication presumes content, container, and media of communication; thus, communication fidelity is closely connected with architecture, process, protocol, and format of the various components.

Characteristics of communication:

- Correct: Is the transmission correct?
- Clear: Is the transmission accompanied by noise?
- Consistent: Is the transmission consistent?
- Complete: Was the transmission complete without disruption or interruption?
- Certain: Is the transmission data source authentic?
- Confirmed: Has the transmission data source authenticity been confirmed?

E.3 Information

Information is corpuscular, quantifiable, morselized, commoditized, objective and "out there," transferable, interconvertible, transparent, autonomous, and measurable. It has shape and can be processed and accessed, generated and created, transmitted, stored, sent, distributed, produced and consumed, searched for, used, compressed, and duplicated. Information can also be of different types with different attributes. It can be sensitive information, and qualitative or quantitative information. Modern uses even extend its use to biological cells using and transmitting information, with cancers, for example, seen as spreading misinformation.

Information is a message that contains relevant meaning, implication, or input for decision and/or action. Information comes from both current (communication) and historical (processed data or "reconstructed picture") sources. In essence, the purpose of information is to aid in making decisions, and/or solving problems, or realizing an opportunity.

Characteristics of information:

- Reliability: Can the source of the information be trusted to deliver reliable information?
- Accuracy: Have the data inputs been captured "first hand," or have they been filtered? Is there any reason to think that there might be any deception involved? Is the source able to communicate the data precisely? Is the source truly competent and knowledgeable about the information they provide? Do they have a known vested interest, hidden agenda, or other bias that might impact the information's accuracy? Can the source's data be verified by other sources or otherwise triangulated?
- Ease of access: What is the financial opportunity and time cost to access the source? Is this the best use of limited resources, or can equivalent data be gained with lesser expenditure? Does the source speak the right language, or will translation be needed?

It is a comparative unit of cognition that defines a change between the previous and present state of natural, artificial, or semantic systems. Businesses often compare data from two different periods of operations. Accounting systems often compare actual performance with standards.

E.4 Concept

Existence of concept presumes a language; ontology is defined in terms of concept(s) and relations between the concepts. It is a perceptive unit of cognition that generates thoughts or ideas that create our intuition and intention—a sense of direction.

E.5 Knowledge

Knowledge is the cognition or recognition (know-what), capacity to act (know-how), and understanding (know-why) that resides or is contained within the mind or in the brain. The purpose of knowledge is to better our lives. In the context of business, the purpose of knowledge is to create or increase value for the enterprise and all its stakeholders.

Within the field of knowledge management, there exist two quite distinct and widely accepted types of knowledge: tacit and explicit. Tacit knowledge is knowledge that is hard to encode and communicate. It is ephemeral and transitory and "cannot be resolved into information or itemized in the manner characteristic of information." Further, tacit knowledge is personal, context specific, and hard to formalize. Toward the other end of the scale, explicit knowledge is exactly that kind of knowledge that can be encoded and is transmittable in language, once again, via the conduit metaphor. It is explicit knowledge that most current knowledge management practices try to, and indeed are able to, capture, acquire, create, leverage, retain, codify, store, transfer, and share.

Characteristics of knowledge:

- Assumptions: This is the knowledge that individuals take for granted. This can come in the form of any of the previously described categories and may refer to things that have occurred in the past, present, or can be fairly safely predicted as going to happen in the future. Explicit assumptions are those that are consciously adopted by the analyst, are well understood, and are shared. Implicit assumptions are those that individuals in the analysis process do not consciously elicit, share, or articulate, and may not even be aware of. Valuable as they are, as with perceptions and beliefs, assumptions need to be consistently and constantly challenged to reflect changing situations and a shifting competitive landscape.

- Facts: Verified information, something known to exist or to have occurred. These are unambiguously true statements and are known to be so. Facts come in any form and will be found among virtually any source of data that enters an employee's awareness or the enterprise's communication and information systems. It is surprising how few enterprises subject their collected data and information to fact checking and verification processes. This becomes even more important for strategy decision-making purposes because many of the facts about competitors and competition are time-sensitive. What may be accurate today may be dangerously incorrect tomorrow.

- Perceptions: Perceptions are impressions or opinions that fall short of being facts, but which are supported to some extent by underlying data or logic. These are often expressed as thoughts or opinions which are put to test to convert them into facts, pending which they have to remain as perceptions for the time being. There is nothing wrong in factoring perceptions into the analysis process, just as long as everybody knows that this is what they are. The error comes when perceptions are mistakenly regarded and treated as facts when they are not. The use of perceptions is perhaps the most exciting element to subject to subsequent analysis, especially when using scenario analysis, war-gaming, what-if analysis, and other such future-oriented techniques.

- Beliefs: Beliefs are often drawn from a mix of facts and perceptions and commonly describe cause–effect relationships. They can be either explicit or implicit, but they too need to be subjected to verification and justification. Beliefs often color the way individuals understand their world and the way in which they think about the future. Therefore, it becomes critical in the analysis process for beliefs to be aired and made transparent to those individuals who are key parts of the process, whether these individuals are data gatherers, analysts, or decision makers.

- Projections: Projections are composed of a mixture of assumptions, facts, perceptions, and beliefs. They are justified or substantiated judgments about the future. It is again important that the analyst be able to powerfully defend or justify their projections as they become a critical part of the knowledge base underlying the decisions made.

- Synthesis: Having identified the type of knowledge in place, the analyst can proceed with greater confidence toward a high-quality output. Qualified inputs are then subjected to the real heart of analysis—the thinking processes, sifting, synthesis, induction, deduction, abduction, experimentation, mathematical conceptualization, experimentation, research, application of methods, techniques, and a vast array of other activities all designed to generate unique and actionable insights.

E.6 Intelligence

Intelligence requires ability to sense the environment, to make decisions, and to control action. Higher levels of intelligence may include the ability to recognize objects and events, to present knowledge in a world model, and to reason about the plan for the future. In advanced forms, intelligence provides the capacity to perceive and understand, to choose wisely, and to act successfully under a large variety of circumstances so as to survive, prosper, and reproduce in a complex and often hostile environment.

Intelligence is thought or mental processing capacities:

- Learning—pattern recognition, memorizing, recalling, correcting mistakes, and sensemaking
- Conceptualizing—modeling, prioritizing, and categorizing
- Analytical thinking—analyzing, interpreting, understanding, scenario playing, and evaluating
- Critical thinking—logic and reasoning
- Creative thinking—imaging, imagining, supposing, hypothesizing, and simulating
- Quick thinking
- Performing—reading, speaking, music, physical activities, and so on
- Problem solving, decision-making, and judging
- Affective thinking—emotion handling

E.7 Wisdom

Wisdom means more than being cultured and well educated; it implies an ethical obligation to improve society and an attitude of caring. While intelligence is related to action, wisdom is related to options and how to judge what we should do. Therefore, wisdom is making (human) sense of data, communication, information, knowledge, and intelligence, and is composed of values and vision.

Characteristics of wisdom:

- Reasoning ability (has the unique ability to look at a problem or situation and solve it; has good problem-solving ability; has a logical mind)
- Expeditious use of information (is experienced; seeks out information, especially details; learns and remembers and gains information from past mistakes or successes)
- Sagacity (considers advice; understands people through dealing with a variety of people; feels he or she can always learn from other people; is fair)
- Learning from ideas and environment (attaches importance to ideas; looks at different perspectives; learns from other people's mistakes)
- Judgment (acts within own physical and intellectual limitations; is sensible; has good judgment at all times; thinks before acting or making decisions)
- Perspicacity (can offer solutions that are on the side of right and truth; is able to see through things—read between the lines; has the ability to understand and interpret his or her environment)

Wisdom is a pragmatic unit of cognition that generates volition—a chosen way of acting and communicating. Wisdom is the process of choosing ordered routines, intended to achieve success and eliminate obstacles.

References

M. Arnaboldi, G. Azzone and M. Giorgino, *Performance Measurement and Management for Engineers* (Elsevier, 2015).

E. Barrows and A. Neely, *Managing Performance in Turbulent Times: Analytics and Insight* (Wiley, 2012).

B. Brijs, *Business Analysis for Business Intelligence* (CRC Press, 2013).

G. Cokins, *Performance Management: Integrated Strategy Execution, Methodologies, Risk, and Analytics* (Wiley, 2009).

W. W. Eckerson, *Performance Dashboards: Measuring, Monitoring, and Managing Your Business* (Wiley, 2006).

J. Fernández, E. Mayol and J.A. Pastor, Agile Approach to Business Intelligence as a Way to Success in A. A. R. El Sheikh and M. Alnoukari Eds., *Business Intelligence and Agile Methodologies for Knowledge-based Organizations* (IGI Global, 2012).

A.N. Fish, *Knowledge Automation: How to Implement Decision Management in Business Processes* (Wiley, 2012).

J. L. Harbour, *The Performance Paradox: Understanding the Real Drivers that Critically Affect Outcomes* (CRC Press, 2008).

J. C. Henderson and N. Venkatraman. (1993). Strategic alignment: Leveraging information technology for transferring organizations. *IBM Systems Journal*, 32(1), 4–16.

T. Hill, *Manufacturing Strategy: Text and Cases* (Palgrave, 2014).

M. H. Hugos, *Building the Real-Time Enterprise: An Executive Briefing* (Wiley, 2004).

W. Jiang, *Business Partnerships and Organizational Performance* (Springer, 2014).

V. Kale, *Guide to Cloud Computing for Business and Technology Managers: From Distributed Computing to Cloudware Applications* (London, UK: Auerbach Publication, 2015).

V. Kale, *Agile Network Businesses: Collaboration, Coordination, and Competitive Advantage* (CRC Press, 2017).

Kaplan, R. S. and D.P. Norton, (1992). The Balanced Scorecard: Measures that Drive Performance. *Harvard Business Review*, (Jan–Feb): 71–79.

R. S. Kaplan and D. P. Norton, *The Balance Scorecard: Translating Strategy into Action* (Harvard Business Review Press, 1996).

J. Koralun-Bereźnicka, *Corporate Performance: A Ratio-Based Approach to Country and Industry Analyses* (Springer, 2013).

S. Karadgi, *A Reference Architecture for Real-Time Performance Measurement: An Approach to Monitor and Control Manufacturing Processes* (Springer, 2014).

W. Kaydos, *Operational Performance Measurement: Increasing Total Productivity* (CRC Press, 1999).

B. Kuhlin and H. Thielmann Eds., *The Real-Time Enterprise-Facts and Perspectives* (Springer, 2005).

J. W. Martin, *Measuring and Improving Performance: Information Technology Applications in Lean Systems* (CRC Press, 2010).

D. Metz, *The Concept of a Real-Time Enterprise in Manufacturing: Design and Implementation of a Framework based on EDA and CEP* (Springer Gabler, 2014).

M. W. Meyer, *Rethinking Performance Measurement: Beyond the Balance Scorecard* (Cambridge University Press, 2002).

A. Neely, *Business Performance Management Unifying Theories and Integrating Practice* (Cambridge University Press, 2nd Ed., 2007).

A. Neely, C. Adams and M. Kennerley, *The Performance Prism: The Scorecard for Measuring and Managing Business Success* (Prentice-Hall, 2002).

P. R. Niven, *Balance Scorecard Step-by-Step: Maximizing Performance and Maintaining Results* (Wiley, 2nd Ed., 2006).

P. R. Niven, *Balance Scorecard Evolution: A Dynamic Approach to Strategy Execution* (Wiley, 2014).

M. Peterson, *An Introduction to Decision Theory* (Cambridge University Press, 2009).

E. S. Pound, J. H. Bell and M. L. Spearman, *Factory Physics for Managers: How Leaders Improve Performance in a Post-Lean Six Sigma World* (McGraw-Hill, 2014).

M. Rist and A. J. Pizzica, *Financial Rations for Executives: How to Assess Company Strength, Fix Problems and Make Better Decisions* (Apress, 2015).

T. L. Saaty and L. G. Vargas, *Models, Methods, Concepts & Applications of the Analytic Hierarchy Process* (Springer, 2nd Ed., 2012).

O. Shy, *Industrial Organization: Theory and Applications* (The MIT Press, 1995).

A. Simon, *Enterprise Business Intelligence and Data Warehousing: Program Management Essentials* (Morgan Kaufmann, 2014).

Z. Tang and B. Walters, The Interplay of Strategic Management and Information Technology in A. W. K. Tan and P. Theodorou (eds.), *Strategic Information Technology and Portfolio Management* (IGI Global, 2009).

J. Taylor, *Decision Management Systems: A Practical Guide to Using Business Rules and Predictive Analytics* (IBM Press, 2011).

S. Tonchia and L. Quagini, *Performance Measurement: Linking Balanced Scorecard to Business Intelligence* (Springer, 2010).

K. Verweire and L. Van Den Berghe, *Integrated Performance Management: A Guide to Strategy Implementation* (Sage Publications, 2004).

D. Wade and R. J. Recardo, *Corporate Performance Management: How to Build a Better Organization through Measurement-Driven Strategic Alignment* (Butterworth-Heinemann, 2001).

Index